ESSAYS IN
MUSICAL ANALYSIS

By

DONALD FRANCIS TOVEY

IN SIX VOLUMES

*The last volume containing a Glossary
and Index and some additional notes*

CONTENTS

ESSAYS IN
MUSICAL ANALYSIS

By

DONALD FRANCIS TOVEY

REID PROFESSOR OF MUSIC IN THE
UNIVERSITY OF EDINBURGH

Volume IV

ILLUSTRATIVE MUSIC

LONDON
OXFORD UNIVERSITY PRESS
HUMPHREY MILFORD

OXFORD UNIVERSITY PRESS
AMEN HOUSE, E.C. 4
London Edinburgh Glasgow New York
Toronto Melbourne Capetown Bombay
Calcutta Madras
HUMPHREY MILFORD
PUBLISHER TO THE UNIVERSITY

FIRST IMPRESSION	1936
SECOND IMPRESSION	1938
THIRD IMPRESSION	1941
FOURTH IMPRESSION	1943

PRINTED IN GREAT BRITAIN

CONTENTS

WEBER

SCHUBERT

BERLIOZ

MENDELSSOHN

SCHUMANN

WAGNER

SMETANA

JOACHIM

DVOŘÁK

RIMSKY-KORSAKOV

PARRY

JULIUS RÖNTGEN

ELGAR

RICHARD STRAUSS

BANTOCK

J. B. McEWEN

ERNEST WALKER

VAUGHAN WILLIAMS

REGER

GUSTAV HOLST

A. VOORMOLEN

PAUL HINDEMITH

CXXXVI. INTRODUCTION TO VOLUME IV

THIS volume deals with music which, being under no compulsion to adapt its habits to words, actions, or ceremonies, confesses itself to be descriptive independently of circumstances. Such a confession need not prevent it from justifying itself as absolute music; but the terms 'programme music' and 'the Romantic School' are applied to music that confesses; while music that does not confess is called 'absolute' and 'classical'. The fashionable revolt against romanticism has already subsided into a patronizing tolerance, and our neo-classical composers are striving to become as 'non-representational' as our sculptors, painters, and stage artists. These are hard matters and too high for me.

The contents of the present volume are, like those of the other four, selected by the accidents of concert-giving under difficulties, but the resulting lacunae here become especially grotesque. I am asked why I have nothing to say about Mahler. A Reid Concert is the only mechanism that will extract an analytical essay from me; and I will deal with Mahler as soon as my orchestra is established with six horns and fourfold wind. Boiling oil awaits me for my neglect of Berlioz in Vols. I–III (where he has no possible place) and red-hot pincers thereto for my irreverence to him in the present volume. My doom was sealed when, the other day, in writing about Gluck I 'revived the exploded fallacy that Berlioz's technique was defective'. I revived no exploded fallacy; Berlioz's technique is as unquestionably defective as beri-beri is a disease of defect in the vitamins. The defects are neither punctilios for pedantry, nor signs of immaturity or struggle; they are not wrestlings like the harshness of Beethoven's counterpoint, nor youthful exuberances like the redundancies of Schubert, nor primitive squalors like the counterpoint of Gluck and of Handel's cook. They are ordinary students' blunders. Schumann wisely remarked that any correction of them merely substitutes a banality for a trait of character. This is true of the work of most intelligent beginners. They all begin with a Berliozian style of harmony; but invincible ignorance was not the only quality of Berlioz's genius.

Parry's Overture to an Unwritten Tragedy would have taken its proper place beside Brahms's Tragic Overture if Vol. II had not been made up before the concert at which I gave it. And no classification is worth the inconvenience of breaking the series of Beethoven's symphonies and Brahms's orchestral works in order to put the Pastoral Symphony and the Academic Overture into the present volume.

B

CXXXVII. 'FALSTAFF', SYMPHONIC STUDY, OP. 68

Since I wrote this analysis the composer kindly gave me permission to correct it by comparison with his own commentary, which appeared in *The Musical Times* of September 1st, 1913, and which, to my shame, I had not read. But my delinquency has its advantages; for it gives rise to a unique opportunity for demonstrating how far a great piece of 'programme music' can be intelligible as pure music and at the same time convey the subject of the composer's illustration to other minds without the use of words. Accordingly I have retained my analysis with all its mistakes, and have corrected it by the composer's analysis in footnotes marked (E). This initial must not be taken to make the composer responsible for the wording of the footnotes; but it implies his authority for their substance. On the whole I am quite satisfied with my success in guessing the composer's literary meaning. Glaring failure about main points would be as unsatisfactory from the composer's point of view as from mine; for my impressions are those of a musician, and not those of a dilettante who might be excused for all manner of blunders in appraising musical values. Where I am wrong I do not see how I could have guessed right, but I have no difficulty in seeing the composer's point when his account corrects me.

Prophecy about the judgement of posterity is as otiose a game in matters of art as in other matters of history. But I have sometimes been compelled to investigate works of art that I should not care to revive; and I have never found in a perishable work anything like the signs of greatness and vitality that abound in Elgar's *Falstaff*. How its musical values can ever diminish I cannot see. To prove the greatness of a work of art is a task as hopeless as it would be tedious; but, like the candidate who failed in geometry, I think I can make the greatness of this one appear highly probable.

Let me begin by 'blowing the expense', and for once giving a tolerably complete list of thematic quotations. With thirty-three musical examples I have to omit any theme or incident that does not recur outside its first context; hence, any theme that appears only or always in continuity with a quoted theme, and any variation that can be described in words or easily recognized on a first hearing. Even so, I could describe several passages more easily with the aid of another six quotations.

This enormous mass of definitely different themes is about equal to that of Beethoven's Eroica or Ninth Symphony; and Elgar's work is one continuous movement, not essentially interrupted by its two intermezzi. It is completely independent of the Lisztian doctrine that all the themes of a symphonic poem should be derivable from a single thematic cell or *Urkeim*. The plausibility of that doctrine lies in the fact that a ripe and highly intellectual musical style tends to develop fascinating thematic connexions as a form of wit. The fatal weakness of the doctrine is that such wit does not concern the foundations of musical composition at all, and is not necessarily more logical than a series of puns. Speaking without the composer's correction, I see and hear no musical reason why these thirty-three quotations should prove to have any thematic relations beyond those to which I draw attention. But in the art of composition the work coheres like a diamond. Its clarity is the crystalline artistic simplicity that comes from the enormous pressures of an inexhaustible imagination; not from the weary eliminations of a taste that declines from one boredom to the next. It is not a matter of previously ascertained form; nor is it a matter of literary illustration.

To the task of musical illustration Elgar brings the resources of a mind long ago well and deeply read, and especially replenished for the matter in hand. He is of the classical race of *attentive* artists; his view of his literary subject will be intensely his own, because his mind will be concentrated upon it. Hence his musical illustrations will amount to a close symbolical tissue, like those by which Bach, Mozart, and Beethoven habitually illustrate words when illustration is called for. Nevertheless I do not propose to analyse *Falstaff* from this point of view. I know neither this music nor the two parts of *King Henry the Fourth* well enough to do so; and in the nature of the case the music is (as Mendelssohn urged in a very profound argument on musical illustration) much more definite than words. And it so happens that Shakespeare has not given Sir John to us in a connected narrative at all, but in a series of episodes deftly but by no means closely wrought into an historic pageant, which is another series of episodes with little more coherence than that of popular history. But, strange to say, it is just in the management of such pageantry that the capacity for composition is most severely tested. Elgar's *Falstaff* is as close and inevitable a musical structure as anything since Beethoven; and this cannot be claimed for *Henry the Fourth*. But for *Henry the Fourth*, alike in the aspects of comedy, chronicle, and tragedy, it can be claimed that Shakespeare's power of movement is at its height; in other words, that the art of composition is omnipresent in that general sense which is more vital than any external form. And here Elgar's power is identical with Shakespeare's, and, being subject to none but purely musical conditions that are its own breath of life, it also achieves a perfect external form. One of the essential characteristics of that form is the combination of weighty symphonic development with episodic leisure and freedom. I hope to show, as occasion arises, how vividly the composer brings before us, by sheer power of abstract form, the contrast between the irresponsible roisterings of the comedians and the ominous background of dynastic troubles.

But I am not going to look for minute details. The particular illustrations I can at present see are obvious enough. I should not be surprised to learn that there were hundreds more; but the composer has not lost grasp of his music in their pursuit, and you and I certainly will lose grasp of the music if we do not attend exclusively to it. When we know both Elgar's and Shakespeare's Falstaff by heart we may amuse ourselves with Gadshill robberies and the arithmetical progression of rogues in buckram. Till then let us be broadly general over the human characters, and attentively musical about details and forms. (By the way, I take it that *The Merry Wives of Windsor* may be neglected. The composer who wishes to put Falstaff into an opera must use *The Merry Wives of Windsor* as the only possible framework of a plot; but the real Falstaff is not there except in one or two good phrases.) Here is unquestionably the real Falstaff, wallowing, protesting, and formidable in his absurdity.[1]

No doubt it may be possible to find the Shakespearian origin of the following pair of satellite themes; but all I know is that one is perky or quizzical, like any Elizabethan page—

and the other scolding, like some aspects of Mistress Quickly[2] or less respectable persons (overleaf).

[1] Not as yet quite absurd but (as Morgann says, writing in 1777) 'in a green old age, mellow, frank, gay, easy, corpulent, loose, unprincipled, and luxurious'. (E.)

[2] Exx. 2 and 3 are among Falstaff's personal themes. 'I am not only witty in myself, but the cause that wit is in others.' (E.)

Ex. 3.

But the later developments of these themes do not fit any particulars of the kind, and Ex. 2 is no subordinate character in the whole work. A counterstatement gives Ex. 1 in the bass below a cataract of trills into which the scoldings have merged. One of the most significant features of style in this work is the fact that most of the themes will make powerful basses, as already shown at the outset by the fact that Ex. 1 stands without harmony. In this respect Elgar may remind us of Richard Strauss, especially as something like the Straussian *panache* is essential to the character of Falstaff. But, with all respect to Strauss, there is more art in *Falstaff* than in *Ein Heldenleben*. The unaccompanied main theme of *Heldenleben* is great; but the problem of its eventual harmonization is contemptuously evaded, whereas Elgar's harmonization never suggests that it was ever a problem at all, whether it consists of a combination of themes or a mass of impressionist scoring. And every one of Elgar's combinations of themes is a statement of excellent harmony made by the combined melodies. The more modern view regards the technical difficulty of this as a restraint. The wiser view recognizes it as a resource. A student with a dangerous sense of humour once brought to my score-playing class some pages of *Falstaff* as a prepared task. He forestalled my comments by explaining that being pressed for time, he had chosen these pages as a 'soft option' because, though for full orchestra, they consisted entirely of two-part harmony. This satisfies Brahms's test with a vengeance, the test of covering up the middle of the score in order to see what the top and bottom is worth 'without trimmings'.

In the fourth theme of the opening complex we clearly recognize Prince Hal in the mood[1] of that soliloquy when he declares his intention of imitating the sun by allowing himself to be hidden in base contagious clouds in order to be more wondered at when he breaks through them.

Ex. 4.

This theme is noble; and the composer would have gone wrong in his musical and dramatic psychology if he had made it otherwise. Breeding will tell, whatever flaws may deface the character. But

---

[1] In his most courtly and genial mood. The symbol of his stern military character will be found in Ex. 28 of the present essay. (E.)

Elgar withholds his accolade; this theme is *not* marked *nobilmente*, though that is how it must be played. It is true to the Shakespearian irony, deeper than the Sophoclean, and perhaps less aware of itself than the Euripidean; true to the irony which indulges in popular sentiments with apparent zest until the very groundlings must feel the approach of shame. Shylock and the glorious sport of Jew-baiting; Hamlet and the diverting farce of lunacy; Prince Hal, who owes Falstaff his love, and who has from first to last been stealing the pleasures of disreputable 'ragging' with the deliberate intention of pompously and publicly disgracing his poor dupes as soon as he is crowned; all these things the interpreter of Shakespeare should give us with the illusory side foremost. The poet's deeper views may be subversive, but the uneasy censor will discover nothing but impenetrable popular orthodoxy.

The continuation of Ex. 4 is broadly melodious and based on different material which I do not quote. Its counterstatement is followed by a re-entry of Ex. 1 in violas with a sinuous counterpoint in the 'cellos. Suddenly it turns aside into the remote key of E minor, where a new theme appears.

Ex. 5.

scherzando.

Except in obvious cases, I do not propose to identify themes with persons. But we may go so far as to identify bass registers with male characters. And Ex. 5 lends itself to stratagems and spoils.[1] It is given time to explain itself in square statements and counter-statements. Then the perky-and-scolding complex (Exx. 2 and 3) returns and leads to a grand peroration reviewing all the themes and unobtrusively introducing a new tottering bass to Falstaff.

Ex. 6.

The peroration ends with a descent of Ex. 1 from the top of the orchestra to the bass register of the last bars of the theme. These are reiterated expectantly, with a pause.[2] Now, in a quicker tempo,

---

[1] The rising scale in the latter part of this quotation shows Falstaff as cajoling and persuasive. (E.)

[2] Thus far Section 1, presenting Falstaff and Prince Henry. (E.)

action begins.[1] Still we have to deal with new themes, and not until the fat is in the fire (as might be Falstaff larding the lean earth at Gadshill) do the new themes combine with the old.

First we have a group of four new figures conspiring together in a single sentence.

These are repeated with a new modulation after a pause. A new theme impinges on them, blown up like a bladder with sighing and grief.[3]

It is given plenty of room to vent its grievance; and then the action begins. Both the figures of Ex. 6 are developed in a fugato in combination with Exx. 1 and 5. This quickly leads to a collapse upon Ex. 7, which is thrice insisted on. Then the figures of Exx. 8 and 9 conclude this exposition.

At the present juncture, whatever events may have been so far represented they issue now in a noble outburst of Falstaffian moral indignation.

---

[1] Section II. Eastcheap—Gadshill—The Boar's Head, revelry, and sleep. (E.)

[2] Women, such as the Hostess, Doll Tearsheet, and 'a dozen or fourteen honest gentlewomen'. (E.)

[3] Not at all! 'A goodly, portly man, of a cheerful look, a pleasing eye and a most noble carriage.' (E.)

Ex. 12.[1]

Harmonized grandly in two-part counterpoint, relieved from austerity by occasional faintly heard inner notes, this theme, like many others in the work, is exposed in the manner of a fugue. There are three entries: soprano, alto, and bass. It is important to realize, as Bradley points out, that Falstaff is no coward, either in fact or in reputation. In battle Sir John Coleville surrendered to him on the strength of his name. The object of Poins in the Gadshill plot was to show him up not as a coward but as a boaster. Poins clearly distinguishes him from his two colleagues thus:

'Well, for two of them, I know them to be as true-bred cowards as ever turned back; and for the third, if he fight longer than he sees reason, I'll forswear arms.'

Honour hath no skill in surgery, and Falstaff will tolerate no humbug but himself. I ask the reader to glance ahead to Ex. 17 for the magnificent combination of Exx. 12 and 11, which here follows in a lower key, less convenient for printing in an economical way. Ex. 11 is then continued in combination with the quaver figure of Ex. 7. With a rapid decrescendo the music recedes into distance, and the conspirators, Exx. 7, 8, 9, now plot in whispers. Falstaff (Ex. 1 broken up in a variation alternately with the figure of Ex. 9) is alert but mystified. Something new and innocent makes its appearance.[2]

Ex. 13.

But I am afraid that the Prince is also tiptoeing in the neighbourhood with mischievous intent—

Ex. 14. Outline of Ex. 4.

and though Falstaff in 'diminution' does not seem formidable, I would not trust him with my money.

---

[1] 'I am a rogue if I were not at half sword with a dozen of them two hours together.' (E.)

[2] A cheerful out-of-door ambling theme. (E.)

Ex. 15.   Ex. 1 diminished.

As this mysterious episode develops, the connexion between Ex. 13 and Ex. 4 becomes more obvious. Ex. 12 persists quietly in its course, with evident effort to maintain its nonchalance. But the surrounding darkness is too much for it, and eventually all themes are lost in a passage consisting of ominous rustlings and whisperings. Prince Hal, in a new variation anticipating Ex. 16, is present; another conspirator (Ex. 5, Falstaff himself?)[1] is groaning in the background. The ominous rustlings are resumed with deeper tone; but they suddenly end in a sportive version of Prince Hal's theme, accompanied by running triplets.

Ex. 16.   Variation of Ex. 4.

This is given room to display itself thrice in different keys. Then shrill cries and whistles[2] lead to a fierce fight. Ex. 12, diminished in quavers, hacks its fugal way in A minor with the utmost energy,[3] and soon settles down in E minor to reiterating its first figure with growing emphasis, until it merges into a re-entry of Ex. 10, loud, complaining, and, as before, soon combining grandly with Ex. 11 at its full size, thus—

Ex. 17.

Suddenly this dies away, and Ex. 7, with both its figures, expresses unholy glee in dialogue between various treble instruments. A new theme of syncopated minim chords,

appears softly and timidly above tambourine-sounds of marching steps. At a sudden stand-and-deliver, Ex. 13 reappears, at first with a new full-toned boldness, but it fades out into Ex. 11, plangent as ever, though faint, on muted horns below derisive scales descending in the violins. Falstaff also bestirs himself in diminution (as in Ex. 15), perhaps a little testy under the persistent and monotonous gibes of Ex. 10.

[1] Yes; see note on Ex. 5.
[2] The short struggle for the twice-stolen booty 'got with much ease'. (E.)   [3] The discomfiture of the thieves. (E.)

And now comes one of the most remarkable features in the form of this work. In and around the key of G minor, Ex. 10 occupies no less than fifty-eight bars, thirty-two of which are marked to be repeated.[1] Nothing breaks the monotony of two-bar rhythm, and there are not many breaks in the series of 4-bar or even 8-bar phrases in which the episode runs its course. As with the stiff, antithetic style of Schumann, the interest lies largely in epigrammatic wit. Elgar has temperamentally much in common with Schumann, and at any time in his career he could have made himself as popular as Grieg by abandoning all methods of composition except the rigid mosaic of Schumann's larger works. But such a style ceases to be rigid and becomes a mighty achievement of athletic muscle when it is absorbed into the contrasts of a freely organized work. This episode has, in relation to the rest, exactly the audacity of movement by which Shakespeare carries us through the several scenes in which Prince Hal is wasting unlimited time with his pot-house companions. Among details, notice the combination of Exx. 10 and 5, classically euphonious like all Elgar's counterpoint.

At length Falstaff protests. The solo Falstaff of the orchestra, the bassoon, almost as loud as Coleridge thought it to be, declaims in terms of Ex. 12, *quasi recitativo*. It collapses cynically into Ex. 9, out of which arises a new theme in the chattering staccato of the wood-wind.

Ex. 18.

The composition still maintains its sectional, episodic character while this new theme, together with a complaining, slow chromatic counterpoint, develops into a row. When this has run its course and died away, the former badinage is recapitulated with an effect of insolent regularity, though it is really only epitomized. But it includes Ex. 12 again, although Falstaff's voice, worn out in the singing of anthems, becomes alarmingly wheezy. Soon we hear him sleeping. And though the musical illustration of this is as audible as sleep can be, it reveals, both in itself and in its context, the poetic depth of the whole work. A mere musical illustrator would, even if he failed to show why Falstaff was in hiding behind the arras, certainly have tried to illustrate the exposition of the contents of Falstaff's pockets, and the derision aroused by the famous bill for a ha'porth of bread with an intolerable deal of sack. But the more we study Elgar's Falstaff the clearer does it appear

[1] The 'honest gentlewomen's' theme, now complete and raised to due importance, runs its scherzo-like course. (E.)

that the composer is achieving something lofty, severe, consistent, and far out of the depth of opera or even of drama. He is giving us Falstaff entirely from Falstaff's own point of view. The old rascal is not sentimental; but, as Theobald divined from a corrupt text, ' 'a babbled of green fields' on his death-bed; and Elgar knows that when he slept there was a wistful beauty in his dreams of Jack Falstaff, a boy who could have crept into any alderman's thumb-ring, page to the Duke of Norfolk.

The theme of the 'Dream Interlude' has a purposely indefinite family resemblance to such quizzicalities as Ex. 9; but not even the thread of personality itself can make a solid bridge over the gulf between that dreamland past and the drastic present.[1]

Ex. 19.

Falstaff awakes again to his roistering world.[2] Exx. 2–3 return in full vigour. And now he must play the soldier. I hazard the guess that in the following new complex of themes we may perhaps see Falstaff as recruiting officer, and can agree with his estimate of his mouldy, feeble, warty, and vituline recruits.

Ex. 20.

Ex. 21.[3]

Ex. 22.[4]

Between Ex. 21 and Ex. 22 the contrapuntal combination of Ex. 10 over Ex. 5 intervenes. I know nothing more 'gravity-removing' than the effect of Ex. 22 when it is delivered timidly in musical dumb-crambo by the various thumpers and tinklers known as the 'kitchen' department of the orchestra.

[1] The contrast of 'what might have been'. (E.)
[2] Section III. Falstaff's March—The return through Gloucestershire—The new king—The hurried ride to London. (E.)
[3] A fanfare, once distant, then nearer. (E.)
[4] A fitting accompaniment to the marching gait of the scarecrow army. (E.)

Another theme joins the slouching march and initiates a fugato which gradually develops into a fight (without prejudice to the etymological connexion of fugue and flight).

Ex. 23.[1]

There is also evidence of what Bradley calls 'so ridiculous an object as Falstaff running'. (Combination of Exx. 1 and 6.) But such absurdity, Bradley also implies, is immune, and Falstaff gains credit in battle by frauds which show effrontery rather than cowardice. There are a few more new figures in this battle episode (if such it be), but they do not recur, and the tumult soon dies away. With extraordinary subtlety Ex. 22 becomes a new formal lyric episode, in alternation with Ex. 23.

Ex. 24.[2]

Then, as if the land were once more safe for wayfarers, we renew our acquaintance with Ex. 13, in alternation with a new rustic and reedy motive of laziness.

Ex. 25.

And so we come to Shallow's orchard, where, in another self-contained episode, we listen to tabor and pipe—

Ex. 26.

and indulge in drowsy reminiscences.

Ex. 27.

---

[1] The March. 'I have foundered nine score and odd posts.' (E.)
[2] As we approach the fields and apple-trees the march assumes a song-like character. (E.)

This interlude comes to a definite end: but the drowsy motive of Ex. 26 would fain continue. It is rudely interrupted by a shrill outburst of violins (another new figure), reintroducing Ex. 8. 'Under which king, Bezonian? Speak or die?' Harry the Fifth's the man; and we shall all be augmented in the new fount of honour. (Ex. 12 by augmentation. No extra marks will be awarded to candidates who detect this point.) Exx. 23 and 22 scurry away post-haste into the distance.

After a pause we find ourselves near Westminster Abbey amid solemn sounds betokening the approach of the coronation procession.[1] A new theme—

Ex. 28.

sounds a note of insistent appeal. As it eventually proves to be Falstaff's last death-bed gesture, I presume that it indicates his passionate belief[2] that the king will be to him the beloved prince glorified. Laughter is in the air—

Ex. 29.

and, in another new theme, Falstaff shares in the glow of affectionate loyalty to the new king.

Ex. 30.

(This immediately combines in counterpoint with Ex. 1.) Another theme may be taken to be at least consistent with cheers and the waving of caps.

Ex. 31.

Poor Falstaff still believes that Henry the Fifth is the light fantastic Hal of Ex. 16. So that brilliant variation is the substance of the

[1] Section IV. King Henry V's progress.—The repudiation of Falstaff, and his death.

[2] No. It is the King himself in military character. (E.)

next crescendo, and Falstaff's cheers transform Ex. 31 to its rhythm.

Ex. 32.

The king arrives in all his glory (Ex. 4, *grandioso*, for Elgar still wilł not say *nobilmente*). The cheers are loud, but there is a barrier between the king and his old friends.

Ex. 33.

Falstaff's heart is fracted and corroborate: the joyful whoop at the end of Ex. 28 becomes a bewildered question, and nothing is left for him but disillusioned memories. The rest is easy for the listener to follow, there are no new themes, and the long tale of old themes is given in the form of reminiscence, not development. Here is the tale: Ex. 28 last figure, Ex. 5; pause; Ex. 28 revived; Exx. 12, 5, 21,[1] 31, 33, subsiding into a mournful decline on the subject of Ex. 28; a faint echo of Ex. 33, then the laughter of Ex. 29 at half pace, transformed as if to falling tears; failing memories of Exx. 7, 1, and 5: a long pause; a breath of sleep-laden wind from Shallow's orchard, Ex. 27, disturbed for a moment by the quizzical accent of Ex. 10, now heard for the last time; it melts into pathos, and Ex. 27 declines farther into an entirely unspoilt memory of the prince whom Falstaff loved (Ex. 4, in full, pianissimo and cantabile); then Ex. 1, failing.[2] Mistress Quickly's account of his death is neither more nor less pathetic than Elgar's; but here, as throughout the work, Elgar is giving us Falstaff's own mind, which is far beyond the comprehension of any other character in the play. We may perhaps recognize Mistress Quickly in a mournful cadence of the clarinet just after the fading out of Ex. 1; but up to the last we cannot be sure that we are spectators: the sudden final rally on Ex. 28, with its bold presentment of the remote key of E minor as penultimate to the last chord, will do equally well for a salute from Falstaff to his estranged king,[3] or as an epitaph in praise of his

---

[1] It is the furious fanfare of Ex. 21 which marks the King's sentence of banishment. (E.)

[2] The moment of death is marked here by a full chord of C major pianissimo on the brass. (E.)

[3] The King's stern theme thrown curtly across the picture. (E.)

loyalty. He was a soldier, and, with all his humbug, no coward; so let him go to Arthur's bosom with a roll of muffled drums.[1]

It will not surprise me to learn that every one of my parallels between the music and the particulars of Falstaff's doings and surroundings is wrong, except the illustration of his snoring. About such sounds there can be no mistake; snores are snores whether they are produced by double-basses and a contrafagotto or by the nose; and if the composer does not mean them he ought not to produce them. But I have hopes that this analysis may not be misleading as to the musical form and Shakespeare-Elgar psychology of the work as a whole.

DITTERSDORF

CXXXVIII. SYMPHONY, 'THE FALL OF PHAËTON' (AFTER OVID'S METAMORPHOSES: BOOK II)

1 *Adagio non molto, leading to* 2 *Allegro.* 3 *Andante.* 4 *Tempo di Minuetto.* 5 FINALE: *Vivace ma non troppo presto, ending in* 6 *Andantino.*

Karl Ditters, afterwards ennobled into Ditters von Dittersdorf, was born in 1739, and died two days after the completion of his autobiography in 1799. That autobiography is a delightful and rather touching document, of which an English translation by Arthur D. Coleridge was published by Bentley in 1896. In fiction or history there is no better account of the artistic and social atmosphere of a petty court in an eighteenth-century bishop's palace. Dittersdorf tells us nothing of his symphonies on the *Metamorphoses* of Ovid except that three years before 1786 'it had occurred to me to take some of Ovid's *Metamorphoses* as subjects for characteristic symphonies, and by the time of my arrival in Vienna I had already finished twelve of them. By way of compensating myself for my travelling expenses, I ventured on a speculation with this music of mine, which was attended with such remarkable incidents that I must make rather a long story of it.' The 'long story' contains interesting conversations on music and musicians between Dittersdorf and the Emperor Joseph, which I should be tempted to quote if our subjects were Mozart and Clementi; but the only point in the 'long story' that concerns the Ovidian symphonies is that Dittersdorf profited by the first fine weather to give the first six of them in the open air, and the others a week later at the theatre, and that, after paying for the copying of the parts and for an orchestra of forty persons, he cleared three times as much as his travelling expenses. This is all

[1] No: the drum roll is shrill; the man of stern reality has triumphed. (E.)

very satisfactory, but it does not help us to follow his interpretation of Ovid. As a result of an afternoon's strenuous frivolity in company with the Professor of Humanity, I hope I can state fairly accurately what the music of Dittersdorf's second Ovidian symphony represents.

The first movement is headed by the first line of Ovid's account:

Regia Solis erat sublimibus alta columnis

(OVID, *Met.*, lib. ii, 1)

and describes the Palace of the Sun. Ovid tells us wonderful things about its decorations which represent all things in heaven and earth and ocean, ranging from sparkling stars to great whales. Dittersdorf's music no doubt illustrates this, and probably in so doing judiciously flatters the palace of Schönbrunn, or perhaps even the palace of his patron, the Prince-Bishop of Breslau, Schafgotsch—Carlyle's 'airy, dissolute Schafgotsch'. No quotations are required for the quite normal and solemn introduction and allegro in the style of an early symphony of Haydn.

The slow movement is a charming piece of melody (Dittersdorf's invention in eighteenth-century lyric melody may be ranked very high), headed with the quotation:

Deposuit radios propiusque accedere iussit. (41.)

Phaëton comes to the palace of his father the Sun-god, who lays aside those rays which none who are less than gods can approach, and bids him draw near. The youth speaks of his mortal mother, Clymene, and demands from his father a convincing proof of his divine birth. So far as the Professor of Music and the Professor of Humanity can make out between them, the rude utterances of the strings in octaves present Phaëton in a rather indignant mood; while the beautiful melodies, worthy of Gluck or Haydn, which they interrupt, represent his divine father with his admiration of his spirited son and his tender memories of Clymene. I see no sign of Phoebus's rash oath by the River Styx to grant Phaëton's boon. Dittersdorf could have borrowed Handel's thunder if he had had a drum. In *Semele* a drum-roll indicates the oath by the Styx. At all events, this andante is a charming piece and thoroughly successful as pure music. So is the minuet headed by the quotation:

Paenituit iurasse patrem. (49.)

though it is rather difficult to trace in it the Sun-god's description of the perils of driving the Sun's chariot across the sky with the wild beasts of the Zodiac for sign-posts, and the fearful steepness of the morning climb, the giddiness of the noonday heights, and the need of an arm stronger than Jove's himself to check the evening down-rush. Dittersdorf has, I think, concentrated himself on the paternal character of Phoebus. Certainly the coaxing accents of the trio are very well suited to the style of his pathetic appeal to Phaëton to look upon his anxiety as the surest proof of his paternity. It is worth while quoting the themes of the minuet and trio to show the simple contrasts which to the eighteenth-century composers are so full of dramatic meaning.

We begin to understand classical music when we realize the rhetorical and even theatrical origin of many phrases which we are apt to dismiss as purely conventional. (See Sir Hubert Parry's 'Lectures on the Histrionic Style', *passim*.)

I regret to say that Dittersdorf shirked the most thrilling part of the story, the description of Phaëton's ride; but, as in most of these Ovidian symphonies, his finale abandons regular forms and devotes itself to illustrating the catastrophe. It is headed by this quotation:

> Intonat, et dextra libratum fulmen ab aure
> Misit in aurigam pariterque animaque rotisque
> Expulit et saevis compescuit ignibus ignes. (311–13.)

There are no themes, but the growing danger of Phaëton's course is indicated in a *crescendo* of ominous harmonies which at their climax would be thought quite interesting even in a fairly modern work. I should not be surprised to find the following sequence in Saint-Saëns's *Phaëton*.

After a little dialogue between the plaintive oboes and the rough strings, Jupiter intervenes with the thunderbolt which hurls

Phaëton out of the chariot and out of life, and consumes in its own flames the fierce fire that threatened the world. Dittersdorf could not afford even one kettledrum, to say nothing of Saint-Saëns's triple roll for three players; so the silences before and after the catastrophe are more impressive than the noise. When the ruins of the catastrophe have subsided there is a final andantino, representing Phaëton's sisters, the Heliades, mourning his death and transformed into poplar-trees.

Ex. 4.

SAINT-SAËNS

CXXXIX. SYMPHONIC POEM, 'PHAËTON'

The modern French composer does not encumber himself with an elaborate apparatus either of classical lore or of musical forms when he wishes to illustrate a classical tale. He does not write a symphony in four sonata movements with a correctness of form which Haydn would have rejected as stiff, until in the finale Jove's thunderbolt brings him down like Phaëton, form and all; nor does he head each movement with the appropriate quotations from Ovid. It is not necessary for him that the Sun-god should repent his promise in a minuet and trio. The requirements of musical form can be satisfied with even greater perfection by a strict attention to the most interesting part of the story. All that Saint-Saëns gives as a preface to his score is the following note:

Phaëton has obtained leave to drive the chariot of the Sun, his father, through the heavens. But his unskilled hands mislead the horses. The flaming chariot, thrown out of its path, draws too near to the earth; the whole universe is on the point of perishing in fire, when Jupiter strikes with his thunderbolt the rash Phaëton.

The music starts with the superb gesture of the hapless demigod seizing the reins, and then for a while all goes well.

Ex. 1.

Allegro animato.

There is perhaps a note of false security in the cheerful theme which the brass instruments soon throw in.

Ex. 2.

But the sense of movement remains delightfully easy, as no doubt it did to poor Phaëton himself even up to the very moment of the thunderbolt. Certainly we are allowed a smiling view of the terrestrial regions before there is more than a distant suggestion of coming danger—

Ex. 3.

but by degrees the menacing rhythms of the drums begin to tell by their long continuance as Phaëton approaches too low—

Ex. 4.

Drum.   Compare with Ex. 2.

until with faint strokes on a gong a tragic theme announces the approaching doom.

Ex. 5.

After the thunderbolt the piece dies away in pathetic and broken reminiscences of Exx. 2 and 3 in slow time.

The whole piece is an admirable illustration of what music can do and leave undone in dealing with external subjects. It does not in the least matter whether I am right in identifying Ex. 3 with a smiling view of the terrestrial regions: it may represent the Heliades before they became poplar-trees. This and that detail in the score may be identified with anything else that Saint-Saëns may choose to imagine, or to borrow from Ovid or other poets in connexion with the story. The only thing that really matters is what is so brilliantly carried out—the sense of movement, of hot weather, and of a tragic fall at the end of it. The thunderbolt is of course a somewhat concrete incident, easily identified with the aid of three kettledrums, a big drum, cymbals, and a gong.

MOZART

CXL. OVERTURE, 'DER SCHAUSPIELDIREKTOR' (THE THEATRE-MANAGER)

Der Schauspieldirektor is a one-act comedy, in which Herr Buff engages a troupe for his theatre. He hears several actors and actresses in comic and tragic scenes; then the tragedy queen sends for her husband, who is a tenor; the leading gentleman sends for his wife, a soprano; and, another *prima donna* being already there, a fine quarrel ensues as to who is first. This quarrel the tenor assuages, and, according to the librettist, harmony is restored. (But Mozart knows better.)

Of course, the scheme is an excellent framework for inserting any number of good things from the two fat volumes of stray arias and ensemble pieces Mozart wrote at various times for concerts, for other people's operas, and for singers who wanted something special at later performances of his own operas. And, as a concert-platform is quite a plausible scene for a voice-trial, I hope some day to produce a suitable adaptation and amplification of Mozart's 'Theatre-Manager' in its entirety, and with a really wide and interesting selection of his wonderful stray arias.

The overture and four numbers, which constitute the whole work as Mozart presented it, date from two months before *Le Nozze di Figaro*, and are unsurpassed in all his works for richness and delicacy. The overture is actually more polyphonic than that of *The Magic Flute*, and, though not cast in contrapuntal forms, not less polyphonic than the finale of the last symphony (which I refuse to call by its popular English nickname). But, like that finale, it enables me to economize in musical quotations by giving a single illustration that combines both first and second subjects. I quote from the recapitulation, where the complexity is at its height.

CXLI. OVERTURE, 'LE NOZZE DI FIGARO'

There are at least six themes in this liveliest of overtures. The first and the beginning of the second are shown in Ex. 1.

It is interesting to compare this opening with that of a contemporary opera which was recently revived with some success in London—Cimarosa's *Il Matrimonio Segreto*. Cimarosa begins with the solemn opening chords of Mozart's *Zauberflöte*, only they are all on the tonic instead of being three different chords. He then proceeds as follows—

Ex. 2.

which he repeats a third higher. In about forty bars he arrives at Mozart's ninth bar, and in another twenty at the crash of the tutti. Also he instructs us in the powers of two, beginning with the fact that twice four is eight. Mozart's simple-seeming opening makes its phrases so overlap that Prout and other seekers after symmetry have tried to persuade us that it begins a bar before the first note. If the audience will kindly sneeze or otherwise indicate the real moment of opening, the conductor will start a bar later and all will be square. Such is the progress of musical education since the death of Mozart.

Symmetrical or irregular, the *Figaro* overture allows nothing to stop it. A repeated figure suggestive of an irreverent allusion to Handel—

Ex. 3.

leads without modulation to a quizzical 'second subject', which culminates in a broad melody.

Ex. 4.

&c.

In the autograph Mozart made the returning link-passage lead to a melancholy andante in D minor, 6/8 time, just as in the *Seraglio* overture, where the place of a development is occupied by a minor paraphrase of Belmont's first aria. There is no subsequent trace of this D minor movement in *Figaro*, and Mozart had written only a couple of bars before deciding that it was out of character. So also is anything like a development. The music gaily recapitulates itself. But though it was not going to be bothered with a development, it has plenty of energy for a long coda in which Ex. 3 makes a grand climax.

CXLII. OVERTURE TO 'DIE ZAUBERFLÖTE'

Professor E. J. Dent's book on the operas of Mozart includes all his researches into the origins and purposes of *Die Zauberflöte*; and a remarkable performance that was given of it under his and Mr. Clive Carey's direction at Cambridge some years ago (before

the war) marked a new epoch in the British appreciation of Mozart
in general and of this supreme achievement in particular. It is now
well known that the apparently nonsensical pantomime which con-
stitutes its libretto is, in spite of having been begun with more
trivial intentions, a masonic manifesto with the loftiest motives.
Goethe saw all that it implied, and actually wrote a second part
to it, bringing its historical and political allusions up to date,
and projecting his prophetic imagination into the future. This
second part is by no means a mere scenario, and is well worth
study by those who choose to go deeply into the meaning Mozart's
opera had for persons of a later generation whose culture was not
primarily musical. Mr. Lowes Dickinson's *Magic Flute* is not
concerned with any such literary history; it represents the thoughts
of a poet-philosopher on the present predicament of human society,
and it takes its title from Mozart's opera because the philosopher
was deeply susceptible to music and understands the full range
of Mozart's ideals. In Mozart's masonic fairyland the ideas of
universal brotherhood are realized on no false assumptions of
equality, and no oppression of the lower by the higher. Tamino
and Pamina pass through the ordeals of fire and water and enter
into their kingdom in the light of Isis. The simpleton Papageno,
who knows nothing of all this, and cannot hold his tongue,
nevertheless finds his Papagena when he is reminded to play upon
his glockenspiel instead of hanging himself. In these holy halls
revenge is unknown; the enemy is forgiven, and his doom is that he
has made himself powerless. This spirit is reflected by Mozart in
what is on the whole the greatest of his overtures. He has no
opportunity here for the sublime terror of the introduction to the
overture to *Don Giovanni*, where he foreshadows the music of
the ghostly statue; nor can he produce a dramatic thrill by so
diverting the end of his overture as to lead to the rise of a curtain
on a scene of adventure at nightfall. His task is simply to produce
a formal overture on a grand scale, combining without offence an
almost religious solemnity with the lightness of touch required by
other features of his pantomime. Mozart's overtures are, with little
or no paraphernalia of definite allusions to themes in the operas, so
closely fitted each to its individual purpose that it would be quite
impossible to interchange them. Here the solemn use of trombones and the all-pervading contrapuntal treatment of the opening
subject (itself in fugue) make this by far the most intellectual and,
with all its brilliant cheerfulness, the most serious overture hitherto
written for the stage. Gluck, in the overtures to *Iphigénie en Aulide*
and *Alceste*, had struck a lofty tragic note with primitive means;
but it needed all the power of Mozart to strike a lofty intellectual
note in the overture to a work the serious aspects of which are so

entirely symbolic that it outwardly presents the appearance of a nonsensical pantomime. The only definite allusion to the rest of the opera is in the 'threefold chord' that intervenes between the exposition and the development. This solemn chord, given out by the wind-band three times with pauses, is a masonic signal which is heard at every turning-point in the action.

Among many interesting uncatalogued items in the Reid Library at Edinburgh is a publication by André (the original publisher of many of Mozart's works), consisting of the full score of this overture exactly as it stands in Mozart's autograph, with certain parts printed in red; the red print corresponding to all that in Mozart's autograph was written later than the rest of the score. It so happened that Mozart here used a much paler ink for the filling out than he had for the skeleton score which he drafted first. I here compress into as few staves as possible a passage from the second subject which shows an interesting alteration, where a little introductory run for the clarinet has been suppressed. The pale ink (or red print) I indicate by smaller notes.

CXLIII. OVERTURE, 'LA CLEMENZA DI TITO'

This admirable example of a festival overture should not be allowed to fall into neglect. The opera to which it belongs is Mozart's last dramatic work, the composition of which, undertaken during journeys by coach and at all conceivable odd moments, overlapped with that of *Die Zauberflöte*. A revival of it is possible only at Mozart-festivals of which the object is to represent as nearly as may be his whole work: it is a *pièce d'occasion* rendered all the more infuriating for the amount of good music which it stifles. The drama is supposed to be one of Metastasio's best. This is a pity. Its evident object is to glorify emperors *ex officio*. Titus Vespasian considers that he has lost that day on which he has not made somebody happy. If the day selected by Metastasio is a fair sample, Titus was an inverted Henry VIII or Shah Shahriah, with a quota of three wives a day, whom it was his duty to pardon for determined attempts to assassinate him by the hands of their discarded lovers. Into the mouth of Vitellia, the horridest female that ever disgraced a libretto, Mozart puts his last and almost sublimest aria, *Non più di fiori*, and contrives to get some more good music out of marches and choruses, and one-and-a-half dramatic moments. For the rest he does not exert himself, while Metastasio's machine is grinding its faultless verses; but in the overture he produces a fine piece of musical architecture, in which several festive formulas are put into new shape. The second subject, a very slender affair in airy dialogue for flutes and oboes, set a fashion which Beethoven followed in his *Prometheus* Overture. The carillon scales in the first subject are a picturesque feature, the value of which is enhanced by the fact that the opening does not reappear until after the recapitulation of the second subject, whereupon it forms a noble coda.

CXLIV. ORCHESTRAL DANCES

*Three Minuets from No. 601 of Köchel's Catalogue, composed
5 Feb. 1791—A major, C major, and G major.
Six Waltzes with coda (Köchel No. 567), composed 6 Dec. 1788—
B flat, E flat, G major, D major, A major, C major.
Any number of other sets and selections.*

At the turn of the eighteenth into the nineteenth century the dance music for the public ball-rooms of Vienna (no *Valse des Fleurs* for a Tchaikovsky ballet, but public dance music for the ordinary public to dance by) was, more often than not, supplied by great composers. Schubert's dances are well known; Beethoven's, with some queer things foisted upon his name, are not less well known, and an interesting set dating from his middle period was discovered not long before the war. Weber's are not inaccessible; but Mozart's, which are immeasurably the finest and richest, are unaccountably neglected. It is quite impossible to exaggerate their importance from every point of view. I have cut down my selection to nine. There are some hundred and thirty, most of them written in the last three years of his life, all of them bristling with epigrammatic wit, and orchestrated in a style that puts them absolutely beyond the reach of pianoforte arrangements. Perhaps this is one reason why they are almost unknown. The orchestra is without violas, and there are only two grades of loudness, *forte* and *piano*. On the other hand, the wind-band is extremely varied, and something queer is always turning up; a hurdy-gurdy, a side-drum, a piccolo (really, like all Mozart's piccolo parts, a kind of flageolet), and a set of tuned sleigh-bells are among the items we should need in order to do justice to the whole of Mozart's dance music. With hardly an exception, all the minuets and waltzes are of the same length, viz. eight bars repeated, eight bars repeated; trio the same, and minuet (or waltz) *da capo* without repeats. So the dancers are never put out. But if any one thinks the phrasing is going to be stiff within this tiny square frame, the mistake will soon appear!

Let us not forget that this dance music is no dream of Utopia, but was a bourgeois reality in Vienna a hundred and thirty years ago.

CXLV. MASONIC DIRGE (KÖCHEL'S CATALOGUE, NO. 477)

Mozart took Freemasonry very seriously, and his Masonic music has a religious depth the expression of which is not interfered with by the language of comedy which permeates even the most serious Church music of his time, and makes some of his Masses far more scandalous than those of Haydn, who apologizes to the Almighty for finding worship irresistibly conducive to cheerfulness. The Masonic parts of the *Zauberflöte* have a strange and ethereal solemnity, which profoundly influenced Beethoven, and which no one but Beethoven could reproduce.

The *Maurerische Trauermusik*, or Masonic Funeral Music, was written in 1785, and was probably used on several occasions during Mozart's lifetime, since we find him altering the scoring according to circumstances, replacing the horns by his favourite corni di bassetto, or alto clarinets, which always contribute to the peculiar colour of his Masonic music, and, next to the strings, are the dominant orchestral colour in his *Requiem*. The corno di bassetto is nowadays difficult to procure. It is an alto clarinet with a few extra notes at the bottom, but otherwise with the same fingering as the ordinary clarinet. A modern alto clarinet is now on the market, but with sublime idiocy its makers have omitted to supply the extra low notes which are essential to all Mozart's music for the corno di bassetto; that is to say, essential to the only extant music for the instrument that is worth playing. Fortunately the original single bassett-horn part of the *Trauermusik* is not noticeably different from that of a bass clarinet.

The *Trauermusik* is a short adagio in C minor, of which the beginning and the end are a structure of slow wailing chords on the wind instruments, to which the strings add a flowing quaver accompaniment. This beginning and ending are a frame for a wonderful figured chorale in E flat, where the strings make an accompaniment, sometimes heroic and sometimes lyric, to a Gregorian tone which neither I nor Otto Jahn can precisely identify, but which is closely allied to that of the *Lamentations*.

BEETHOVEN

CXLVI. OVERTURES TO 'LEONORA', NOS. 2 AND 3

THE OPERATIC PRELUDE AND THE PERFECT TONE-POEM

It is a commonplace of criticism to say that the opera *Fidelio* proves Beethoven's ignorance of the theatre; and throughout the second half of the nineteenth century there was overwhelming temptation to those musicians who admitted no dramatic music except Wagner's, to explain away the embarrassing fact that *Fidelio* invariably makes a deep impression in spite of the many obscurities of its libretto and the difficulties of the music. An adequate account of *Fidelio* (or as it was first called, *Leonora*), and its place in Beethoven's art was not to be expected so long as the musical world was divided between Wagnerian martyrs and persons with a conscientious objection to all forms of opera. As for myself, I have been diagnosed as a case of paralysis of mind by an eminent critic who happened to see some notes of mine indicating that *Fidelio* is after all quite a good opera. It certainly is a horribly embarrassing phenomenon for exclusive Wagnerians, and it is an even worse stumbling-block to those abstract-minded musicians who object to all recognition of the rhetorical force of purely instrumental music.

Some writers have even gone so far as to deny that Beethoven's style is dramatic at all; maintaining this position by pointing out that if certain passages in *Fidelio* are dramatic, they are not more dramatic than similar passages in the pianoforte sonatas, string quartets, and symphonies. Such writers are to this extent in sympathy with Beethoven, that they are making the very mistakes that Beethoven made in his first version of his opera. But unfortunately they make them on the assumption that dramatic expression in instrumental music is more reserved and less intense than that of music for the stage. Now we shall never understand the aesthetics of opera (nor even of instrumental music) until we realize that dramatic expression on the stage is merely more immediately effective, and that it is in the interests of intensity and concentration that 'absolute music' demands conditions untrammelled by the stage. If we once fix our attention upon the right illustrations, this ceases even to appear paradoxical. Few things in opera are more effective, for instance, than the short passage at the beginning of *Don Giovanni* where the Commendatore is killed. Is the passage too highly pitched in rhetoric for a symphony? Would it, if introduced into a symphony of Mozart or Beethoven, throw the rest of the work into the shade or seem exaggerated in tone? On the contrary, the passage is precisely the sort of thing Mozart wrote in his symphonies at the age of twelve, where it sounds as dry and without atmosphere as the corresponding thing in slabs of scene-painting would look if transported from the stage to the walls of an academy exhibition. The real objection to theatrical art when it is removed from the theatre is always that it is sketchy and bald. The tremolos that have such a fine gruesome effect in the incantation scene in *Der Freischütz* sound ridiculous when Weber introduces them into a piece of chamber music. When Beethoven attacked, somewhat late in life for a first opera, the problems presented to him by *Fidelio*, he encountered a most unlucky combination of circumstances and influences, which his own dramatic instincts served only to aggravate. He was too much in revolt against the eighteenth century to appreciate a comedy of manners. This unfortunately meant that the one supreme master of opera from whom he could have learned exactly what he needed was the one whose libretti most scandalized him. If only Mozart had lived to come, as Beethoven did, under the influence of Cherubini, and to take up the romantic style which was arising in French opera, then Beethoven might have profited by Mozart's experience.

As it was, the only master from whom Beethoven could learn to set the kind of drama that appealed to him, was Cherubini. With all his mastery and nobility of style, Cherubini lacked precisely that quality of dramatic movement which Mozart had both by instinct and experience, and which Beethoven had already acquired in instrumental music to an extent altogether transcending the possibilities of theatrical music. The strange and touching result was that Beethoven impetuously threw himself at Cherubini's feet, explicitly and personally acknowledging him as his master; a compliment which poor Cherubini could return only by complaining that Beethoven's music made him sneeze. Cherubini's masterpiece, *Les deux Journées*, or *The Water-Carrier*, was based on a tale of a heroic woman, who in a series of thrilling adventures rescues her husband from death as a political prisoner. The author of the libretto had written at least two more libretti on much the same theme. One of these, *Helène* (containing the idea of a trumpet-signal behind the stage as *deus ex machina*), was composed by Méhul; while *Fidelio, ou L'amour conjugal*, was the subject which attracted Beethoven. Here the heroism of the woman and the tragic plight of the prisoner are on a far greater scale than in the other two stories. There were two things, however, which Beethoven did not know. One was that Mozart would never accept a libretto until the librettist had shown himself thoroughly reasonable in threshing out every problem of musical importance to the composer. The other was that the whole French school of opera, of which the Italian Cherubini was by far the greatest master, had long ago completely abandoned (if it had ever seriously tackled) the problem of reconciling musical and dramatic movement, so that all French libretti of that period were designed accordingly. Mozart seems constitutionally incapable of deficiencies in movement. Beethoven is no less incapable of leaving a problem of movement unsolved, though his first sketches may get into difficulties. When he came to compose *Fidelio*, he threw his whole energy into a story the climax of which was highly dramatic and impressive; but it took him nine years, from 1805 to 1814, to find out that the first part of the libretto was designed like a vaudeville, full of absurdities which Mozart would never have allowed to stand. When *Leonora* was first produced the critics complained that words and passages were repeated far too often. It is a touching proof of Beethoven's docility that he, with every natural disposition towards terse dramatic expression, should have been misled by taking Cherubini as his model in this obvious and avoidable defect. In the final version of *Fidelio*, as produced in 1814, Beethoven secured the services of a more experienced craftsman to revise the libretto; and the result was at last a fairly coherent and consistent work of art, though there are still some obscurities left in the first act, particularly in the complete lack of motive for the music to interrupt the dialogue where it does, or for the dialogue to interrupt the music.

But the most impressive result of Beethoven's nine years of meditation on the subject of this opera that had cost him so much thought, is the fact that the *Leonora* overtures, which had been inspired by the heroic climax of the last act, proved to be too great for use in connexion with the opera at all.

Indeed, it is difficult to see how Beethoven ever brought himself down to the love affairs of the jailer's daughter as an opening to his first act, after such a tremendous prelude as the *Leonora* overture was, even in its first version. The first version is of course that known as *No. 2*. *Leonora No. 1* is the latest of the three overtures of that name, and is on entirely different material. Being the smallest, it is by far the most suitable for connexion with any but the final version of *Fidelio*, for which Beethoven in 1814 composed the one entirely suitable prelude. The overture to *Fidelio* in E major, dramatic, brilliant, terse, and with an indication of some formidable force in the background, is in just the right tone to indicate that there is something serious behind the pretty comedy of Jaquino and Marzellina on which the curtain rises. In fact, by 1814 Beethoven had learnt the musical values of the stage. In 1805 he had his instincts, which were undoubtedly theatrical as well as dramatic; but not even the endless vexations of the production of his opera could enlighten him as to their true cause, and in 1806 very little of the extensive revision which he gave to the work was better than mutilation and makeshift. Not until the libretto was severely taken in hand by an expert in 1814 was it possible for Beethoven to get to the root of the matter, where the composition was remediable at all. In the meantime the one thing that really profited by the revision of 1806 was the overture; but it profited in a fatal way, which raised it to one of the greatest instrumental compositions in existence, and at the same time ensured that it should absolutely kill the first act. This is how Weingartner comes to find that *Leonora No. 2* is an eminently successful dramatic introduction, while *Leonora No. 3* is a great concert-piece. It is not because *No. 3* is less dramatic than *No. 2*. The trouble with *Leonora No. 3* is that, like all great instrumental music from Haydn onwards, it is about ten times as dramatic as anything that could possibly be put on the stage. Here again we must discriminate.

Sir George Grove got into extraordinary difficulties in connecting *Leonora No. 3* with the subject of *Fidelio* at all, probably for no other reason than that he was so deeply impressed by it as a piece of instrumental music. Unfortunately he tried to give his reasons, and gave some of the worst the mind of man could devise. He argued that the subject of the rescue of a prisoner from a petty country jail was too small for so wonderful a composition, and that the least one could think of was the sufferings of a beleaguered city. Grove must have understood music and life better than to believe in this argument himself. If there is one thing certain about art and life, it is that the heroic acts or sufferings of the individual are as big as the mind can hold, and that the horrors and heroisms of a besieged city are not emotionally cumulative. Beethoven found the heroic devotion of Leonora, the faithful wife, a more inspiring subject than any romantic story of young love, or any general catastrophe of war. He knew as much as most civilians about war, and if in those Napoleonic times a subject had been brought to his attention which (like the siege of Weibertreu)[1] implied the heroic devotion of a thousand faithful wives, he would still have seen that the sublimest artistic treatment of that subject would consist in taking a single case.

Let us now compare the two great *Leonora* overtures on this basis, that both are inspired by a theme which Beethoven rightly considered sublime, and that they are not related as a sketch and a finished product, but that the earlier is definitely a theatrical prelude, while the later is, though Beethoven did not at first realize the fact, an ideal piece of instrumental music. Otherwise we shall get into a hopeless tangle if we regard the alterations in *Leonora No. 3* as of the nature of criticisms of *No. 2*.

Introduction. The first alteration is in the first bars, which in the earlier version begin with what Grove, in his Irish vein, called a 'false start'.

Ex. 1.
No. 3.
Adagio.

That is to say, the figure (*a*) is given separately in *No. 2* before being embodied in the long descending scale. But the listener who has never heard any of the *Leonora* overtures before, must be gifted with a spirit of prophecy if he takes that very emphatic opening of *No. 2* for a 'false start'. When Beethoven wrote *No. 2* he must have meant (*a*) as a definite figure and the long scale as a development of it. And when we inquire into the meaning of this figure (*a*) we find that it foreshadows Florestan's aria, which, after a mysterious modulation to the distant key of B minor, enters in A flat, the key in which it is to appear in the opera when Florestan sings memories of his wife and his 'fight for truth' that brought him to die in chains and darkness.

[1] Weibertreu is the town where the conqueror allowed the women to go free with such property as they could carry on their backs. So they carried their husbands. Classical poetry prefers the single parallel case of Aeneas and Anchises.

As the quotation shows, the two overtures differ in the details of this melody; and they also differ from not less than three other different versions which Beethoven made for Florestan's aria.

The omission of the first three notes of *Leonora No. 2* of course obliterates the reference to figure (*a*), and is highly significant as showing how little Beethoven relies on thematic connexions as a means of construction.

The continuation of Florestan's theme is a wonderful series of remote modulations on figure (*a*). The first six bars are in *No. 3* compressed from the vast but regular eight bars of the earlier version. The next five bars, where (*a*) appears in the bassoons and basses, with light triplets in dialogue between violins and flute, are compressed from ten bars of a much more elaborate and exciting passage in *No. 2*, leading in both cases to a tremendous crash of the full orchestra on the chord of A flat, while the violins rush up and down in gigantic scales. In the earlier version this crash is repeated (with a change of harmony) after a bar's silence, and in this slow time such a silence is surprisingly long. Beethoven then follows the second crash by fortissimo short chords, each at a bar's distance. But in *Leonora No. 3* he does not wish his introduction to be so gigantic or even so impressive. He approves of his earlier material, but prefers to state it in a less startling way. It is enough for him that the new version should cover the same ground as the old in key and phrase, without indulging in effects that leave no room for growth to unexpected climaxes later on. So he has only one great crash in A flat, and fills up the gaps between the short fortissimo chords by quavers on the woodwind.

Then follows a passage on the dominant of C as a preparation for the allegro. In *No. 3* it is five bars long, and is founded on a phrase (*b*) that forms the staple of the earlier part of the development in the allegro. The corresponding passage in *Leonora No. 2* was fourteen bars long, and, though closely resembling this in character and outline, was not sufficiently definite to be made the subject of allusions later on. Lastly, Beethoven alters into something much more normal the amazingly impressive notes which in *No. 2* led to the allegro with dark mysterious colouring.

Altogether his revision of his introduction is not pleasing to that habit of mind which studies works of art from one fine point to the next, and neglects to consider them as wholes.

Allegro. The opening of the allegro, up to the end of the second subject, is substantially the same in both versions, except that Beethoven skips four bars wherever he can. In the *crescendo* that continues the theme, Beethoven leaves out four bars at the beginning, in order to put in a fortissimo delay of four bars just where we expect the climax. Then, as the full orchestra takes up the theme, Beethoven takes the opportunity of keeping up the fortissimo more continuously in *No. 3* than in *No. 2.* Example 4, which in *No. 2* interrupts the tutti by its appearance *piano* on the 'cellos, is in *No. 3* given by the full orchestra.

In the passage that follows in *No. 3* he allows *pianos* and *fortes* to alternate rapidly, instead of the fortissimo of *No. 2*. And it is important to note that he uses triplet tremolo quavers in the first version throughout his tuttis, thereby showing that he was thinking of a slower tempo than that which is obviously right in *Leonora No. 3*. This difference of tempo is of the utmost importance in performance; and throughout *Leonora No. 2* we need to remember that Beethoven knew nothing about *No. 3* until he came to write it.

The passage leading to E major for the second subject is much shortened, and much louder and less mysterious, in the later than in the earlier version; and the second subject itself is re-scored beyond recognition by the eye, though to the ear it is much the same in both overtures. It begins with a transformation of Florestan's aria, with wonderful remote modulations—

and though the scoring of *No. 3* is much easier and simpler than in *No. 2*, the later version will be seen to divide the melody between instruments on different planes. The sequences and subsidiary themes that follow grow at once to a fortissimo in the earlier version, but in *No. 3* they are given intensely, quietly, and mysteriously, only at the last moment coming to a fortissimo as they approach the great syncopated scale-theme, suggested, no doubt, by (*a*).

The quotation shows how the wood instruments in *No. 3* are following the syncopated theme on the beat, a feature which is not found in *No. 2*. Moreover, *No. 3* disposes of the theme in eight formal bars, whereas *No. 2* continues discursively for seventeen. *No. 3* ends its exposition with a little cadence theme of two bars in which the horns are answered by the full orchestra, and this is followed by a descending sequence for the violins alone, which leads quietly without a break into the development, the change to the minor mode being one of the well-known romantic moments in *No. 3*. All this is very different from *No. 2*, which has substantially the same two-bar cadence theme in quite different scoring, but continues in a triumphant forte, ending in a sustained note followed by a remote modulation, that marks off the development from the exposition by a typical *coup de théâtre*.

At this point *Leonora No. 3* takes leave of *Leonora No. 2*, and has no more in common with it (except the idea of the trumpet-call behind the scene) till we come to the coda. We may still, however, find it profitable to contrast the two versions, as the differences are as unexpected as ever. The mind that lives indolently on fine passages and special effects will find even more to regret here than in the revision of the introduction. The development of *Leonora No. 2* begins, as we have said, by a *coup de théâtre* which plunges us into F major. From this point Florestan's aria is carried on in rising sequences alternating with plaintive dialogues on figure (*d*) until the key of D major is reached. Here the whole first theme, as at the opening of the allegro, bursts out in the violoncellos, leading to G major. (This use of the dominant in the course of the development has a very happy effect; how happy Beethoven himself did not realize until at quite a different point in *No. 3* he raised it to a sublime level.) At the present stage (in *No. 2*) the violoncello continues with Ex. 5, which is taken up by the woodwind; and now follows a series of mysterious and remote modulations, mostly pianissimo, with an intensely characteristic episodic figure in the bass and wood-wind, and a sustained level of lofty inspiration that entitles it to a place among Beethoven's grandest conceptions.

Ex. 7.

In *Leonora No. 3* Beethoven, with a self-denial almost unparalleled

in art, writes as if all this had never existed. He founds all the
earlier part of the development on a very large and simple sequence
of great orchestral crashes of single chords sustained for four bars,
alternating with quiet plaintive eight-bar phrases, founded on
figure (*b*) of the introduction (see Ex. 3), combined with (*c*) of
the first subject. To this combination is added, as we proceed, a
development of figure (*d*) like that already mentioned in *No. 2*.

Ex. 8.

Five long steps of this process lead, with a short crescendo, to
a stormy tutti in which figure (*c*) of the main theme is imitated
between violins and basses in rising sequence. In twenty bars this
leads, with a rush of ascending scales, to a pause on B flat; and a
trumpet-call is heard behind the stage. In *Leonora No. 2* the storm
breaks out quite suddenly after a much longer and almost entirely
pianissimo development, and it is worked up for forty-four bars
before closing with the trumpet-call, which is more florid and in
the key of E flat; a not very remote key, and less startling than
B flat, which is of all possible keys the most opposed to C major.

We are now about to learn Beethoven's motives for his stern
rejection of all the finest features of *Leonora No. 2*. The young
author who was advised to strike out all his finest passages would
hardly have had that advice given him if they had been as fine
as those Beethoven rejected. Beethoven's motives are not those
that prompted that advice; he has struck out his finest passages
because he needs room to develop something finer. The fact is
that *Leonora No. 2* is too gigantic up to the present point to be
worked out within the reasonable limits of an orchestral piece in
classical style at all. After the trumpet-call Beethoven makes no
attempt to treat the rest of it on the same scale, but simply brings
in Florestan's aria in C major in its original form (*adagio*, 3/4), and,
without attempting any such thing as a recapitulation of the first
and second subjects of the allegro, goes straight on to a coda,
which we will compare in due course with its vastly larger version
in *Leonora No. 3*. Continuing now with *No. 3*, we have, in the
surprising key of B flat, the trumpet-call of the watchman on

the tower, warning the scoundrel Pizarro that the Minister has arrived to investigate his unlawful detention of his own private enemies in the state prison of which he is governor; and that therefore it is too late for him to put Florestan and his heroic wife out of the way. The flutes and clarinets sing the melody which accompanies Florestan's and Leonora's breathless exclamation: 'Ach! du bist gerettet! Grosser Gott!' (There is no trace of this passage in *No. 2*, though the material for it was already present in the opera.)

Ex. 9.

(I number the bars in fours, so as to indicate the rhythm. Some analysts identify the first four notes with (*c*) of the main theme. I cannot believe in distant thematic references that contradict the rhythmic sense; and even when external evidence shows that they have some foundation, the lesson of the first bars of the introduction is surely that these things are often of no importance in the composer's own mind.)

The trumpet-call is given again (a little louder, according to the direction in the opera); and the song of thanks re-enters in the remote key of G flat, leading very slowly and quietly to G major. We are now beginning to learn a lesson in proportion. Beethoven has, by his compressions and alterations, gained a hundred bars, or nearly a third of the bulk up to the trumpet-call. *Leonora No. 3* reaches that point in 236 bars as against the 335 of *Leonora No. 2*. He has thus left room to grow; and so he continues his development at leisure, with a sunshiny passage in which the flute and bassoon give in G major the substance of the tutti that followed the first subject, from which Ex. 5 was quoted. This is the sublime and unexpected use of the dominant to which I referred in connexion with the development of *Leonora No. 2*. Suddenly all is still, except for the strings climbing upwards with figure (*c*). Then there is a perfectly unadorned rising slow chromatic scale in octaves, leading with immense deliberation to the above-mentioned tutti (omitting Ex. 5), fortissimo in the tonic as at first. This does duty for the recapitulation of the first subject, and leads at once to the second, which is given in full, with no alteration except the necessary transposition to the tonic. The syncopated scale theme (Ex. 8) leads straight to the coda, which begins with Florestan's aria once more, as in the second subject.

This corresponds roughly with the adagio that followed the trumpet-call in *Leonora No. 2*; but the gain in not changing the tempo is immense, and the passage is much expanded so as to keep us long in suspense.

Ex. 10.

Again we may note that the alteration obliterates the original connexion between the last notes of the Florestan figure and the sequence of scales with which the peroration begins. The idea in *No. 2* is to turn the last notes of the theme into a staccato scale passage, capable of making an effective short crescendo in the original allegro tempo, so as to lead quickly to a brilliant final presto. The idea in *No. 3* is that of a whirlwind of sound, presto from the beginning, twice as long as the earlier passage, and relying upon its intrinsically exciting quality of sound in a way which makes any question of its derivation merely pedantic. The logic of the excitement is rather to be sought in the enormous breadth of the coda to which it leads. In *No. 2* the first theme bursts out presto in a diminution. This is to say, that besides being presto, it is also rhythmically twice as fast, with quavers for crotchets. In *No. 3* there is no doubt that this would not do, though after the first two bars the framework is for some time the same in both overtures, the scoring being brighter and less bustling in detail in *No. 3*. Soon we come to the syncopated scale theme (Ex. 7). *No. 3* first gives it for eight bars pianissimo instead of being part of an unvaried fortissimo as in the early version. It gains still greater breadth in *No. 3* from the fact that it is now for the first time prolonged, whereas in *No. 2* it was already as long when it first occurred at the end of the second subject.

The tremendous passage that follows in *No. 3*, leading through another and even more deliberate slow chromatic scale to a really terrific climax on a chord of the *minor* ninth, is entirely new and makes the rejected grandeurs of *No. 2* fade into insignificance. This is the very point at which the coda of *No. 2* ceases to aim higher than an interesting theatrical finish. *No. 3*, the grandest overture ever written, then returns to the joyful reiteration of the figure of its main theme, and ends in the utmost height of triumph.

CXLVII. OVERTURE, 'LEONORA NO. 1'

Beethoven's opera was first produced under the title *Leonora* in 1805, with the overture now known as *Leonora No. 2*. In 1806 it was produced again, with alterations that were little better than mutilations, except in the case of the overture, which was expanded into the tremendous symphonic poem known as *Leonora No. 3*. In 1807 a project was mooted for producing the opera at Prague. This came to nothing, but it was probably the cause of Beethoven writing *Leonora No. 1*, which clearly shows that he had already discovered that the former mighty works annihilated the first act of the opera, which begins quietly with apparently trivial matters, and only very gradually prepares for the tense and heroic drama of the last act. Seven years later, when the opera was thoroughly overhauled and largely rewritten as *Fidelio*, Beethoven abandoned the *Leonora* themes altogether in the new overture, with which he at last achieved the perfect introduction to his first act.

Leonora No. 1 thus represents an interesting middle stage in Beethoven's treatment of the *Fidelio* problem. It also shows amusing signs of the irritation which the whole business of the opera had caused him in 1805 and 1806. When performers were careless in any respect, Beethoven was apt to give them a severe lesson by writing something calculated to betray their weaknesses. The singer of the part of the villain Pizzaro was conceited, so Beethoven asked him if he could sing the following passage at sight—

Ex. 1.

Bald krüm-met sich der   Wurm,   bald krüm-met sich der   Wurm!

Of course, it seemed perfectly easy; but when Pizzaro found that he had to sing it against the following figure in the whole orchestra—

Ex. 2.

then the worm *did* begin to squirm!

The orchestration of *Leonora No. 1* is full of similar disciplinary measures, though none quite so atrocious. For the rest, it is an admirable opera-overture, with a broad and quiet introduction containing several distinct ideas: an energetic and terse allegro—

Ex. 3.

with a second group expressive of anxiety and suspense—

Ex. 4.

and with an extensive meditation on Florestan's aria in the dungeon, to replace the development of the overture and to foreshadow the central situation in the opera.

Ex. 5.

CXLVIII. OVERTURE TO 'FIDELIO'

Of all the new parts of *Fidelio* none deserves greater reverence than its overture. The mere act of renouncing that mightiest of all overtures, *Leonora No. 3*, is enough to inspire awe. Beethoven was obviously right; *Leonora No. 3*, even in its earlier version (*Leonora No. 2*), referred entirely to the climax of the story in the last act, and was utterly destructive to the effect of the first act. The only chance for the first act of the opera lies in its conveying the impression of a harmless human love-tangle proceeding between certain good-natured young people connected with the jailer of a fortress governed by the villain. Grim forces are thus manifest in the surroundings, together with a growing sense of mystery about one of the persons in the love-tangle—Fidelio, the disguised wife of the unnamed prisoner, who is rescued by her heroism, when she has helped to dig his grave in the dungeon where he has lain in darkness for two years. A music that reveals Leonora's full

heroic stature (like the overture *Leonora No. 3*) simply annihilates
the first act. In the *Fidelio* overture Beethoven achieves what the
first act requires. A formidable power, neither good nor bad except
as it is directed, pervades the whole movement, and in the introduction alternates with a quiet pleading utterance—

Ex. 1.

which is soon lost in the darkness of Florestan's dungeon, until,
after the drums have entered with slow footsteps, it emerges and
leads into the active daylight of the allegro.

Ex. 2.

This is worked out in sonata form with a terseness and boldness
which is more akin to Beethoven's 'third period' than is commonly
realized. The 'second subject' is in the dominant, as usual, and
contains several short new themes, of which I quote the first—

Ex. 3.

in order that the listener may more readily note a remarkable
feature of form in this overture which occurs in the recapitulation.

The development is short and quiet, the drums bringing back
the main theme dramatically. In the recapitulation an unexpected
turn of harmony brings the 'second subject' (Ex. 3) into the dark
remote key of C major, in which the trumpets, hitherto confined to
repeating a single note on the only chords which admitted it, come
into their own and dominate mightily. Then at last, with a return
to the key of E, the trombones blaze out as the full orchestra breaks
into Ex. 1. The ensuing adagio passage is adorned with a graceful
new triplet figure, and soon bursts into a brilliant final presto.

Throughout the overture the scoring is of Beethoven's most subtle and, at the same time, powerful order; and in its form great issues, dramatic and musical, often hang upon a single bar.

CXLIX. OVERTURE TO 'CORIOLAN', OP. 62

It does not greatly matter that the *Coriolanus* for which this overture was written is not Shakespeare's, nor a translation or adaptation of Shakespeare's, but an independent German play, by Collin. That poet was a contemporary of Beethoven. His plays fill some dozen volumes and, if his *Coriolan* be a typical example, show him to be a master of smooth verse, determined to allow nothing to happen on the stage that can be described in narrative, and to let no consideration of action or movement prevent each character from uttering all the noblest sentiments that the occasion and person inspire. From Collin's play Beethoven derives the vacillating development and the abrupt final collapse of this overture. Collin's Coriolanus finds excuses for delaying the attack upon Rome until the moment at which he can effectively commit suicide. Both plot and denouement are eminently un-Shakespearian; but even Collin, as well as Beethoven, had read Shakespeare, who breaks through like Nature in Beethoven's music. Wagner then, in that analysis of this overture which is one of his finest and most attractive prose works, did well to ignore everything but Shakespeare and Beethoven. No doubt all unauthorized attempts to name descriptive details in 'programme music' will rouse the healthy opposition of those who want to give or withhold names themselves; yet if ever one piece of music could correspond to one dramatic scene, Wagner was right in describing Beethoven's overture as a musical counterpart to the turning-point in Shakespeare's *Coriolanus*, the scene in the Volscian camp before the gates of Rome (Act v, sc. iii). Here, after every political embassy has been dismissed with the annihilating contempt of the banished conqueror, whose figure, as Wagner says, is presented to us with the first notes of the music—

Ex. 1.

there come to him ambassadors against whom his pride struggles in vain.

Ex. 2.

Thence follow restless doubts and delays:

Ex. 3.

Wagner rises to heights of original poetic power in his profoundly true description of the vicissitudes of agonized pleading [Ex. 3], and the fierce pride that breaks the hero, body and soul, before it yields. Wagner's analysis cannot be shortened without injury; but the gist of it may here be indicated in Shakespeare's own words. In the concert-room Beethoven will say the rest, and readers and listeners may perhaps then do the better justice to Shakespeare when they read *Coriolanus*, or at least this scene of the fifth act, at home. Most of us will agree with Wagner, that music has comparatively little to do with politics, human as these may be in the hands of Shakespeare; and in any case it is a mistake to suppose that a single piece of music, especially so terse a movement as the *Coriolanus* overture, could represent the various aspects of a whole play. Even in Beethoven's own opera, *Fidelio*, he at first wrote an overture which referred exclusively to the stirring events of the last act; and when, in his final revision of the opera, he realized that the gigantic tone-poem we know as the overture *Leonora No. 3* totally eclipsed the quiet opening scenes, he based the present overture to *Fidelio* entirely upon the moods and suggestions of the first act.

Here, then, is the beginning of Shakespeare's analysis of Beethoven's *Coriolanus*—

ACT V, SC. iii.

COR.   Fresh embassies and suits,
Nor from the state, nor private friends, hereafter
Will I lend ear to. [*Shout within.*] Ha! what shout is this?
Shall I be tempted to infringe my vow
In the same time 'tis made? I will not.
(*Enter, in mourning habits,* VIRGILIA, VOLUMNIA, *leading young* MARCIUS,
VALERIA, *and Attendants.*)
My wife comes foremost; then the honour'd mould
Wherein this trunk was fram'd, and in her hand

The grandchild to her blood. But out, affection!
All bond and privilege of nature, break!
Let it be virtuous to be obstinate.
What is that curtsy worth? or those doves' eyes,
Which can make gods forsworn? I melt, and am not
Of stronger earth than others. My mother bows;
As if Olympus to a molehill should
In supplication nod; and my young boy
Hath an aspect of intercession, which
Great nature cries 'Deny not'. Let the Volsces
Plough Rome, and harrow Italy; I'll never
Be such a gosling to obey instinct, but stand
As if a man were author of himself
And knew no other kin.

And this is the end—

       (*Holding* VOLUMNIA *by the hand, silent*.)
       O, mother, mother!
What have you done? Behold! the heavens do ope,
The gods look down, and this unnatural scene
They laugh at. O, my mother! mother! O!
You have won a happy victory to Rome;
But, for your son, believe it, O! believe it,
Most dangerously you have with him prevail'd,
If not most mortal to him.

CL. OVERTURE TO 'EGMONT', OP. 84

1 *Sostenuto ma non troppo, leading to* 2 *Allegro, leading to*
3 *Allegro con brio.*

One of the problems that haunts the lover of the rarer products of
theatre-music is how to do justice to Beethoven's *Egmont* and
Mendelssohn's *Midsummer-Night's Dream*, when Goethe's play is
unknown outside Goethe's and Beethoven's country, and is even
there kept on the stage-repertoire avowedly because of the music;
while the theatre-goers of Shakespeare's country have for centuries
frustrated the best efforts of theatre-musicians by maintaining a
rooted belief that theatre-music is divinely ordained to be the
worst music that money can be stinted upon. Even opera-goers
have hardly learned to wait for such things as the last chord of the
first act of *Tristan and Isolde*, a wonderful chord for trumpets
behind the scene, long known in the British Islands only to readers
of the score. Yet opera-goers are in a fair way to become as musical
as concert-goers; and some day play-goers may treat fine incidental
music to Shakespeare not less respectfully than we now treat
Wagner.

The overture to *Egmont* is theatre-music. Like the overture to *Coriolanus*, it does not deal with the whole play, though I am unable to find (as Wagner found in *Coriolanus*) any one scene which covers the ground of the whole overture. But a comparison is possible. Wagner was right in saying that while the political themes of Shakespeare's *Coriolanus* were not musical, Beethoven found inspiration in the conflict of the hero with the not less heroic mother and wife, who vanquish his pride. With *Egmont* the balance is reversed. Clärchen is, indeed, a figure of eminently musical pathos, both in her heroic temper and her incapacity to move mountains by it; and if Goethe could have done for her what Turgenev did for the sparrow that died of heroic rage in the successful effort to frighten a big dog away from her helpless young, then Beethoven could have given more development to the feminine note in this overture. What Beethoven can do for it he does with noble poetic power in the second subject of the allegro, where fierce reminiscences of the introduction alternate with pleading notes, and yield to a glorious remote modulation.

Ex. I.

For the rest, Goethe has not achieved his best with the Clärchen-Egmont-Brackenburg affair. What inspires Beethoven's overture is not the rather sketchy individual characters of the play, but just that political aspect that can furnish so little of musical import in *Coriolanus*. The scene of the drama is in Brussels; and the deliverance of the Netherlands was a more inspiring theme than the persons of Goethe's play. History tells us that when Egmont was on the scaffold Alva took the precaution to drown his farewell speech in the fanfares of a military band. Whether Goethe is alluding to this fact, I cannot say; but it is a fine irony of poetic justice that Duke Alva's fanfares have come down to us as the Symphony of Victory with which Beethoven, following Goethe's behest, sends Egmont to his death. This symphony ends the overture as well as the play; and its meaning is fully explained in the last scene. To Egmont, asleep in prison, appears a vision of Freedom, with the face and form of Clärchen. She shows him that his death will achieve freedom for the Provinces. She acknowledges him victor, and offers him a crown of laurel. She holds it hovering over his

head. A distant drum is heard, and at its first faintest sound the
vision disappears. The sound grows louder. Egmont awakes;
daylight is glimmering in the prison. Egmont feels in vain for
the crown—

'The wreath has vanished! Fair vision, the light of day hath banished
thee! Yes, it was they; they were become one, the two sweetest joys of
my heart. Divine Freedom borrowed the form of my love: . . . She came
to me with blood-stained feet, the swaying folds of her garment stained
with blood. It was my blood and the blood of many a noble. No, it was
not shed in vain. March on, brave nation! The goddess of Victory
leads you! And as the sea breaks through your dykes, so break, so tear
down the tyrant's rampart and whelm the drowning tyranny away from
the ground it arrogates to itself!' (The drums approach.) 'Hark! Hark!
How often this sound called me to march in freedom to the field of
battle and victory! How blithely my comrades trod the path of danger
and glory! I, too, march from this dungeon to an honourable death: I
die for the Freedom for which I lived and fought, and for which I suffer
in sacrifice.' (The background is filled with Alva's soldiers.) 'Yes, bring
them together! Close your ranks, you scare me not. I am used to stand
spear against spear, and, surrounded by menacing death, to feel with
redoubled pulse the courage of life.' (Drums.) 'Thy enemies encompass
thee on every side! Swords flash: Friends, raise your courage! Behind
you are your parents, wives, children! And *these*' (pointing to Alva's
guards) 'are driven by the empty word of their ruler, not by their own
spirit. Guard your possessions! And to save all that you hold most
dear, fall joyfully, as I give you the example.'

Ex. 2.

CLI. OVERTURE FOR THE NAME-DAY OF KAISER FRANZ, OP. 114

This work does not deserve to be neglected; and when it is 'revived',
it should be so played that it can be heard. As far as custom can
be imputed to such rare events as its performance, it is customarily
played far too fast. Weingartner has remarked that, whereas he
takes the finale of Beethoven's Seventh Symphony at an unusually
moderate pace, he is constantly told, sometimes in praise and sometimes in blame, that nobody else has ever taken it so terrifically
fast. Things will always sound fast when every rhythmic unit
bristles with detail. But if we increase the pace until the rhythmic
units become a hum, the listener will sleep like a top.

The *Namensfeier* overture is a short and energetic work consisting of a majestic introduction and a bustling *allegro quasi vivace*. (Note the precautionary *quasi*.) The majesty of the introduction and the sledge-hammer power of climax in the allegro bring this work into spiritual alliance with the mighty *Weihe des Hauses*, op. 124. Eight years passed between the two works; *Namensfeier* being written in 1814, the year of the revival (and revision) of the opera *Fidelio*, and *Weihe des Hauses* being written in 1822. The themes of *Namensfeier* are almost in the nature of short formulas designed to display vivid contrasts of colour and phrase-rhythm without attracting attention to themselves. There is nothing perfunctory in the work: like the overture to *Fidelio* (a work of the same date) it is microscopically perfect in detail. Romantic, however, it does not claim to be, except in so far as there is romance in the impulse of a crowd of loyal subjects to greet their sovereign in his progress through the streets of his capital. Beethoven's tremendous sense of movement was still under the impulse of his Seventh Symphony, and his interest in imperial Name-days was official rather than personal. The crowd interested him more; and after the maestoso introduction has worked its pair of themes (a phrase in loud rhythmic chords and a broad cantabile tune) into a spacious exordium, the rest of the overture suggests an excited and joyful rumour, beginning in whispers and adding information gathered from many different quarters, until the glad news is confirmed and the populace rush together from all sides. No definite 'programme' can be or need be erected from this basis, but such is the mood of the allegro, which is in very terse sonata form with many abrupt little themes, a short development, and a coda which is by far the largest section of the whole work.

An interesting point in the history of the first theme—

Ex. 1.

is that the repeated quaver figure (*b*) was first thought of as a crotchet-and-quaver figure identical with (*a*). Nottebohm is probably right in thinking that Beethoven changed it because he did not like to use in this overture a figure so prominent in the scherzo of the Seventh Symphony which he had just produced.

The transition to the second group of themes is effected by the old Italian practical joke of treating the mere home-dominant chord as if it were the dominant key.

Ex. 2.

But in the recapitulation Beethoven sheds a new light on the old joke by taking it literally. Instead of admitting that those chords were merely *on* the dominant he substitutes tonic chords, with the air of correcting the former mistake.

Ex. 3.

It is strange, but a fact, that this drastically simple stroke in connexion with one of the most hackneyed of structural devices is quite unique.

Less unique but more romantic is the following impressive detail in the scoring of another short and simple phrase. The phrase is stated three times, with a sustained inner dominant throughout. The first statement is on violin and violas in octaves, and it closes into a repetition by flute, clarinet, and bassoon in three octaves. An oboe and horn sustain the dominant throughout. Against this, during the second statement, the strings add a seventh, three octaves deep, with a crescendo and an excited uprush.

Ex. 4.

The overture is full of such typical traits of Beethoven's style. Another great moment is the sudden hush and unexpected move to the subdominant just at the moment of returning to the recapitulation from Ex. 1. The many incidents which thus fleet by almost too rapidly for the ear, make this overture one of Beethoven's most difficult orchestral works. It does not sound difficult; and if its points are missed either by performers or listeners, no disaster is felt, except by those who have had leisure to study the work. It is an eminently 'practical' work, that does not, like the *Fidelio* overture or the Fourth Symphony, court disaster by risky passages. A perfunctory performance can do no worse than make it sound like a perfunctory composition. But if we compare it with a really perfunctory work like the *König Stephan* overture, the difference will soon appear. The harder you work at *König Stephan*, the slighter it becomes; and slight without the engaging frivolity of the *Ruinen von Athen*, but with the insolence of a master who really can't be bothered with such official functions. Beethoven was under no illusions about these patriotic *Festspiele*. The eminent critic, Rochlitz, devoted one or more articles in his musical journal to rebuking Beethoven for becoming increasingly stagey in these works. Beethoven's legitimate defence might have been that as Kotzebüe's *Ruinen von Athen* and *König Stephan* were the flimsiest of stage spectacles, staginess was the only quality admissible in their music. Instead of this reflection he scrawled upon the margin of his copy of Rochlitz's journal some unprintable remarks as to the relative value of Rochlitz's highest thoughts and his own *piéces d'occasion*. But he implied that his own opinion of these pieces was much severer than Rochlitz's. And the *Namensfeier* overture is not among these pieces, for though its opus number (114) is earlier than that of *König Stephan* (Op. 117), it was written three years later. And the sketches show great care.

WEBER

CLII. OVERTURE, 'THE RULER OF THE SPIRITS'

Rübezahl is an early unfinished opera which Weber began in 1808. The fairy tale on which the libretto is based was never a very promising subject for an opera, and ought in any case to have produced nothing more powerful than a Christmas pantomime. In the deplorable absence of any standard edition of Weber's works it is impossible to give a first-hand account of what exists of the opera, though there is little doubt that, as in the later operas, Weber must have intended almost every bar of his overture to have some reference to the music of the drama. The extant fragments of the opera are said to be immature and not very characteristic of Weber. In 1811 the opportunity of a concert in Munich inspired him to remodel the overture with such success that he declared it to be the most powerful piece of work he had yet done. In this form it remains one of his finest compositions; and it is incomparably greater in conception than any possible musical illustration of the story of the poor wizard whose captive princess cheated him into counting the turnips in his garden while she escaped with the aid of a friendly griffin. So we may profitably refrain from all further speculation about the meaning of this piece as programme music. It would be very difficult to guess that this work had not been composed some fourteen or fifteen years later, when Weber was at the height of his power. Although it is comparatively neglected, it is as effective as any concert overture in existence. It is certainly of some consequence in the history of music, for Wagner did not entirely escape its influence in his overture to *The Flying Dutchman*. It has a great wealth of themes, always, as in all Weber's instrumental music, put side by side in sharp contrast, with transitions executed by a *coup de théâtre*. The number of different themes is surprising, and it may save words boldly to quote six of them.

Exx. 5 and 6 represent the second subject; and it will be seen how the calm cantabile of Ex. 6 is ominously disturbed by the 'cello with its agitated interpolation of Exx. 4 and 1. The return of Ex. 5 in the tonic major on the brass instruments is one of the most successful pieces of pioneer work in the history of orchestration. It would be impossible to guess by the sound of it that this glorious mass of soft harmony for brass instruments was written with the imperfect resources available in the year in which Beethoven was writing the *Ruins of Athens*.

CLIII. OVERTURE, 'DER FREISCHÜTZ'

The overture to the most famous of Weber's operas is especially remarkable for the completeness with which it sums up all that music can tell of the story to be enacted. Weber, as usual, wrote it after the opera was finished. At the first performance it aroused such a storm of applause that the opera could not proceed until the overture was repeated. Yet the rest of the opera proved still more convincing, and revealed the real poetic power of the overture. The opera has had its ups and downs in respect of fashion; and we shall never quite recover that part of its romantic thrill that depends on genuine vestiges of superstitious horror, such as Weber's contemporaries felt. But we have by this time also got over the period of contemptuous reaction from such sentiments of horror; and we can therefore appreciate the art with which Weber treats the whole apparatus of his libretto. Edinburgh audiences, moreover, are in the fortunate position of having recent memories of a local revival of the work. It is interesting also to note that it has aroused a refreshing enthusiasm in Berlin, contrary to the fears of critics who prophesied that no *blasé* modern audience could listen to it without hostile merriment. But the truth is that, as Dr. M. R. James has proved, the old-fashioned ghost-story, without any psychological jargon or up-to-dateness, is the most thrilling kind of all. It is the old traditional kinds of spook that are really gruesome; and Weber and his librettist knew the old traditions too well to make any mistake about them.

Max (or, for purposes of English singing, Rodolph), once the finest marksman in the forest, has mysteriously lost his skill, and is in despair. Caspar, his treacherous friend, tells him that on the night of a total eclipse of the moon it is possible to cast seven 'free-bullets' in that accursed spot, the Wolf's Glen. These bullets never miss their mark. What Caspar does not say is that the seventh bullet is guided by the fiend-huntsman Samiel, and that Caspar is gaining respite for himself by delivering Max into Samiel's hands. Samiel will direct the seventh bullet to the heart

of Max's bride, Agathe; and Max's despair will deliver his soul to
Samiel. But Agathe is under the protection of a saintly hermit who
stands by her at the fatal moment. The seventh bullet, baulked of
its mark, claims Caspar, who dies with a curse. Max confesses his
guilt, and is promised pardon when he shall have redeemed himself in a year of probation.

The overture begins with a sound-picture of the depths of
a forest. A lyric melody for four horns drifts in slow regularity,
and dies away into a dark chord—

Ex. 1.

which indicates the fiend Samiel. The despair of Max (*Doch
mich umgarnen finstre Mächte*) underlies the main theme of the
allegro—

Ex. 2.

and the first tutti foreshadows the storm that closes the scene
in the Wolf's Glen.

Ex. 3.

Ex. 4.

A summons from the horns and a passionate slow melody on
a clarinet tell, in one of the most famous passages in romantic
opera, how Max first looks down into the awful depth of the
Wolf's Glen by the light of the full moon, as yet uneclipsed. Then
we hear the main theme of Agathe—

Ex. 5.

In the development, which is, for Weber, very fine and concentrated, Ex. 4 is worked up in an excellent imbroglio. Agathe's
theme penetrates the gloom and is mocked by a horrid echo

from low trombones. This should be gruesome, and not, as Mr. Cecil Forsyth calls it, a 'circus effect'.

At last, after the darkest hour, virtue triumphs and the overture ends brilliantly.

CLIV. OVERTURE TO 'EURYANTHE'

Weber was consumptive from his birth: he had no time to lose, and no desire to waste it. Throughout his thirty-nine years of life, his time was lost for him by fools and humbugs. His master, Abt Vogler, to whom he always remained loyal, was one of the most devastating of musical humbugs. He has been described for all time, not by Browning's poem (to which Browning gave the wrong name on purpose), but by that great classical scholar, Otto Jahn, who in his life of Mozart characterizes Vogler as one of those musical philosophers who disguise their lack of solid musical schooling in a vast ostentation of general culture. Vogler's other great pupil was Meyerbeer. It is a pity the two pupils did not exchange their physical constitutions.[1]

Euryanthe is both a more mature work of art and a more advanced development of Wagnerian music-drama than *Lohengrin*, though it is a generation earlier. No one who knows *Euryanthe* thoroughly will consider this an extravagant statement. There are fully a dozen well-developed leitmotivs waiting for the Wagnerian label-sticker; and the division into set numbers (arias, quartets, &c.) is an illusory survival which could just as easily be foisted upon *Lohengrin*, or even upon *Meistersinger*. While there is nothing quite so sublime in *Euryanthe* as the Prelude and the Grail-themes of *Lohengrin*, Weber remains throughout *Euryanthe* on a level from which he is both morally and technically incapable of sinking as Wagner often sinks in *Lohengrin*. The whole work is of such a quality that a single glance at an unknown fragment of it would convince you that here is the style of a great man; and there is no form of dramatic music—not even the finale, where *Freischütz* itself shows weakness—which is not here handled with freedom and power.

Why then is this tremendous work so seldom heard? Has Lohengrin, in pique at Elsa's want of faith, meanly revenged himself by stealing Euryanthe's birthright? Ask poor Weber what he thought of Frau von Chezy after he had got 'das Chez' to

[1] I have been reproached for the 'savagery' of this wish. It does not seem savage to Weber; and Meyerbeer can afford to put up with it ever since the gentle Rossini said to the composer of a funeral march for that master, 'Would it not have been better if you had died and Meyerbeer had written your funeral march?'

remodel her libretto for the ninth time. Ask him how he came to call his beautiful and virtuous heroine Ennuyante.

He was not the only composer whom 'das Chez' took in. Schubert was another victim. But his *Rosamunde* was only incidental music to a play; and the play being lost, we do not know what it was about, except that she was Queen of Cyprus. It is, however, pretty clear to a musician where the poetasteress's power lay. She had fluent and typical words and images for all moods, and a good sense of contrast. These assets might readily induce a composer to commit himself long before he had time to grumble that her style consisted mainly of indications of the places where style ought to be. This does not often worry a composer whose own style is enough for him. The trouble comes when a great composer like Weber discovers too late that he is devoting the magnificent common sense of his highest structural power to a drama in which the emotions and contrasts, admirably adapted for music in themselves, are associated with events as crazy as the logic of dreams. The beautiful and virtuous Euryanthe is made to appear faithless to her Adolar by means of the treachery of her confidante Eglantine and the villain Lysiart. It is not injured innocence, nor any lofty scruple, nor tragic ignorance, that prevents her from saying the very first thing a rational being would naturally say when first put into her position; it is simply that if she said it the whole story would collapse, and all poor old Chez's verses and all her puppets could not put it together again. For three whole acts all the situations are topsy-turvy: there are no other Gilbertian qualities. Among the most troublesome features of the whole affair are the ghosts of Emma and Udo, who never appear, but who, like the sociable and explanatory ghost in Andrew Lang's *Castle Perilous*, have to bring about the family prophecies, whether the public can follow the rigmarole or not. Well, anyhow, long ago they committed suicide; and Euryanthe, who had to live in a garden adjoining Adolar's family vault, told the dread secret to Eglantine, who told Lysiart, who told Adolar, who saw at once that this proved that Lysiart had won his wager against Euryanthe's truth. Weber did his best for these poor ghosts, and very shrewdly drew public attention to them by bringing the music of their story into the overture, and demanding that the curtain should be raised for a few moments at that point to show Adolar's family tomb.

Such then is the stuff to which Weber devoted the greatest of all his works. In 1922 a distinguished dramatist, Rolf Lauckner, who had the year before collaborated with me and Fritz Busch in the restoration of two Schubert operas, undertook a thorough re-writing of the libretto. Previous attempts have failed through lack of appreciation of Weber's sense of form. It is no use improving the play on lines which imply that Weber's huge musical design matters less than Wagner's. Lauckner's new text alters not a single mood or contrast in the story, and by a constant process of translation from the jargon of 'das Chez' into the language of poetry, achieves a straightforward and impressive drama which perfectly follows and supports Weber's music. In the whole opera no musical addition is required beyond about forty bars, distributed in three separate scenes, the longest interpolation being in one of the recitatives, and the others being in places where the music was patchy as Weber left it. The patchiness was mainly due to the nonsensical dramatic situations, and it vanishes with their removal.

Only one whole number, and two passages (both of them weak) are sacrificed, and only one number transplanted. The rest, or rather the central principle of Lauckner's drama-therapy, consists in his radical reform of the stage-management, so that the eye can understand the situation before a word has been sung. I own that, with all my admiration for the music of Weber's *Euryanthe*, I was astonished at the effect the new text has upon the many tragic and complex passages which suffered from their absurd original background. Correct theories had not sufficed to show that tragic music can be beautiful while the situation on the stage offends the spectator's common sense. It is not necessary that opera should be great literature. It may be as nonsensical as Mozart's *Magic Flute*. But such pantomimes have in a high degree the common sense of stagecraft; and few authors of nonsense can attain the disciplined aesthetic coherence of Edward Lear or Lewis Carroll. The subject and style of *Euryanthe* admits of no nonsense; and it came as a revelation to me to find that Weber's tragic music was worthiest of Beethoven or Wagner just in those passages where the original libretto was incredible. With a truthful text the music reveals its truth. I hope it may not be long before Weber's greatest work is universally recognized in this new light.

The overture begins with one of Weber's brilliant tonic-and-dominant formulas, and then proceeds with Adolar's act of faith.

Ex. 1.

I   trust   in   God   and   Eu - ry - an - the's   love

The whole first subject is in the highest spirits of a brilliant and triumphant court in the age of chivalry. At length the second subject is heralded by a peal of drums and an amorous phrase from the violoncellos. Thereupon enters another of Adolar's themes—his joy at the prospect of meeting Euryanthe.

Ex. 2.

O hap - pi - ness be - yond be - lief

After more passages of heraldic pomp the exposition comes to a climax with a new theme.

Ex. 3.

&c.

The development is preceded by the music of the ghosts in an extremely remote key.

Ex. 4.
Largo.

pp   &c.

Then the lively tempo, somewhat subdued, is resumed with an excellent contrapuntal development of Ex. 3, inverted as follows—

Ex. 5.

pp

With admirable clearness this works out its course and leads to a recapitulation, in which the second subject (Ex. 2) is triumphant throughout. And so to the brilliant end.

CLV. OVERTURE TO 'OBERON'

The history of music in England is full of disasters, being mainly the history of an art that in one phase after another becomes fashionable without achieving much progress towards being understood. Fashion is always delighted with mystery, and suspects common sense of being ill-bred. We are eminently a literary nation, and fashion has found the common sense of our literature too strong for it to outvote; but British men of letters have sometimes been unmusical, and have pardonably judged of music by the fools fashion makes of musicians, whether in its choice or its treatment of them. The fate of English opera during the greatest periods of classical music is a melancholy example. The trouble began when Dryden, utterly disgusted with the type of mind represented by a certain Monsieur Grabu, whose music was the fashion, carefully arranged his 'opera' *King Arthur* so that Mr. Purcell's music should have no connexion with the action or even the characters of the play. Our first and greatest man of genius in dramatic music was therefore condemned to inaugurate a tradition whereby English opera consisted of music that merely added a series of lyric and spectacular digressions to a play which, if good at all, would be better without the digressions. Planché's libretto of *Oberon* represents an advance on this, inasmuch as the play would not be better without the digressions. It could not by any process become worse, except in its taste and moral tone, which are unimpeachably refined. Planché explained to Weber his excellent reasons for conciliating English operatic tastes, and exclaimed after the first performance, 'Next time we will show them what we really can do'. He should not have wasted a whole work in preliminaries. There was no 'next time'.

The librettist has earned a quite respectful mention from literary critics, who are probably surprised (in spite of the example of Metastasio) to find that a man who writes for music can write at all; and no doubt Planché has done better poems or plays than *Oberon*. At present it is only relevant to say that this libretto has murdered the third and last mature opera of Weber, who devoted his dying energies to learning the English language in order to set it. Again and again he implored Planché to send him the whole text, or at all events to give some explanation of the position in the plot of the single pieces, instead of sending mere unexplained airs for the 'tenor' or 'soprano', or ensemble pieces. It was bad enough to have to work thus in the dark; but Weber eventually discovered something worse. He discovered that it did not matter. So he poured his last and finest music into this pig-trough, and shared the applause with the magnificent scenery. Then a Grand Benefit Concert was arranged for a date which the organizers had not noticed to be the Derby day or some such solemnity. Much sympathy was expressed for Weber when on this occasion the public had to be elsewhere. His illness was becoming alarming, and though his leave of absence was at an end, there was no doubt that he was quite unfit for the return voyage. Some friends called on him the morning before his projected departure, hoping to persuade him to postpone it. They found that he had died in the night. He was thirty-nine years old.

Early English editions of *Oberon* are well provided with accounts of the deep feeling which this pathetic event aroused throughout the country, and with the beautiful poems that appeared in the papers. We evidently enjoyed ourselves over this chapter of our musical history.

Like most classical opera-writers, Weber generally wrote the overture after he had finished the opera. He was thus, even in the

case of *Oberon*, able to make the most of the opportunity for de-
fining the moods and foreshadowing the incidents of the drama. In
his greatest work, *Euryanthe*, where the libretto was helplessly
dependent on an ancestral ghost who never even appears on the
scene, Weber actually contrived to make the story clear and effective by raising the curtain to show a tableau in the middle of the
overture. And he had developed the system of leitmotivs fully as
far as the point attained by Wagner some twenty years after in
Lohengrin.

The overture to *Oberon* is, accordingly, full of allusions to the
opera. But these allusions are peculiar, because the libretto is not
even a bad drama (like *Euryanthe*), but the merest twaddle for
regulating the operations of scene-shifters. Weber's fairy-music
has been compared with that of Mendelssohn's music to *A Midsummer-Night's Dream*, to Weber's disadvantage. What is the
use of comparing Planché's fairies to Shakespeare's? Planché's
Oberon has taken a 'fatal vow' to hold aloof from Titania until
he has found a perfectly faithful pair of human lovers. Everybody knows that he only wants an excuse for waving his wand in
order to waft Sir Huon the Bold from Bordeaux to Bagdad in the
twinkling of a scene-shift, and, when Braham the Tenor (I mean,
Sir Huon the Bold) has rescued Rezia the Fair from the un-
speakable Turk, to waft them on to a desert island, bring a pirate-
ship to rescue them, get them sold separately into slavery, and by
these and the like tomfooleries keep them deprived of all human
motives and opportunities for three hours, or until the resources
of the scene-shifters are exhausted. This done, he applauds their
constancy, and tells them that, thanks to them, he now rejoins his
Fairy Queen.

In all this pantomime Weber found three good ideas, which he
promptly turned into traits of genius. I see no evidence that
Planché himself appreciated the importance of these ideas. He
must have expected that Oberon's magic horn would come in
prettily; and no doubt he set great store by the opportunity he
gave Weber for 'Turkish music' as that inspiring Oriental study
was conceived in 1826. It meant simply the use of the big
drum, cymbals, and triangle all together in the rhythm of the
left hand of the major theme in Mozart's *Rondo alla Turca*.
The Turkish music Weber exploited (not for the first time in his
life) very cleverly in its place in the opera; but he did not build
anything important on it. Oberon's horn was different: it was
capable of real poetic power. It can summon Oberon from the
ends of the earth, or herald his approach therefrom. When it
sounds, we see and hear as if space were annihilated; and everything becomes exquisitely clear and tiny, because its immense

remoteness is that of our own inmost soul. Thus, at the end of the opera there is a grand triumphal march at the court of Charlemagne. It is this, and not 'the horns of Elfland faintly blowing', that we hear in *il tutto pianissimo possibile* after Oberon's horn has twice sounded at the beginning of the overture. Through the ignoring of this point, the passage has often been deprived of all its romance by being taken as fairy music instead of very mortal music brought under a fairy spell. Then Weber sounds, in the violoncellos, the note of human love awakening. This, the revelation to Sir Huon the Bold of something better in life than boldness, is the second of the three valuable ideas which Weber extracted from his libretto. The third idea is one which even in its crudest manifestations is a sure mark of greatness in the artist who ventures to use it. It is the conviction that 'the light of common day' is not a thing to be blasphemed. The visions evoked by Oberon's horn vanish with a bang; and all is bustle and pageantry, which the aristocratic composer, thoroughly at home in court-circles, is poet enough to laugh at, but far too well-bred to waste energy in discountenancing.

Again Oberon's horn sounds, and then the clarinet tells how 'A gentle ray, a milder beam Broke sweetly on life's broader stream.' Text-books on instrumentation quote this famous passage either without comment as a piece of orthodox scoring, or with the criticism that a beautiful melody is wasted on a dull region of the clarinet. Both views are misleading. The critical view has the advantage of pointing towards the truth, that whatever Oberon's horn summons comes from the ends of the earth and the depths of the soul. The pianissimo of an immense distance is what should be aimed at here.

The fairy-like and brilliant theme which follows has again no direct connexion with fairies. It is a distant vision of Rezia the Fair on a desert island when she sees the sail of the approaching ship and hails it with her scarf. These then are the principal threads which Weber weaves rapidly and loosely into a gorgeous masterpiece of operatic orchestration. It is more than that. Though the distant visions are, throughout the latter half of the overture, gathered up into a climax of most unfairylike and unsentimental brilliance, yet the last word must be, as I remember Joachim said to me after a performance of the *Oberon* overture at a country musical festival, 'Not a learned composer, but what a poet!'

CLVI. CONZERTSTÜCK IN F MINOR FOR PIANOFORTE WITH ORCHESTRA, OP. 79

1 *Larghetto, ma non troppo, leading to* 2 *Allegro passionato, leading to* 3 *Tempo di Marcia, leading to* 4 *Presto assai.*

Weber's *Conzertstück* is the origin of the post-classical concerto form established by Mendelssohn and followed by Saint-Saëns, and by Max Bruch in his best-known violin concerto. No composer since 1850 would deny the full title of concerto to a work of this range. Like Spohr's *Gesangscene* Concerto, it exemplifies the essentially dramatic, not to say operatic, character that underlies, historically and aesthetically, the concerto as an art-form. But Weber is an inveterate illustrator, whose sense of form becomes liveliest when he has a programme to direct it, as in his overtures. And we know, from the testimony of Weber's pupil, Julius Benedict, what the programme of the *Conzertstück* is. It was told to Benedict on the morning of the first performance of *Der Freischütz*, when Weber played to him this newly finished concerto. 'The Châtelaine sits all alone on her balcony gazing far away into the distance.'

Ex. 1.

'Her knight has gone to the Holy Land. Years have passed by: battles have been fought. Is he still alive? Will she ever see him again?
'Her excited imagination—

Ex. 2.

calls up a vision of her husband lying wounded and forsaken on the battle-field. Can she not fly to him and die by his side?
'She falls back unconscious. But hark!

Ex. 3.

'What notes are those in the distance? Over there in the forest something flashes in the moonlight—nearer and nearer. Knights and squires with the cross of the Crusaders, banners waving, acclamations of the people! And there—it is he!'

Octave glissando from deep bass G to top C of pianoforte.
'She sinks into his arms' (*con molto fuoco e con leggierezza*).

Ex. 4.

'Love is triumphant. Happiness without end. The very woods
and waves sing the song of love; a thousand voices proclaim his
victory.'

Ex. 5.

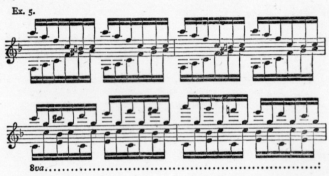

Hollywood needs Weber to teach it its business. We cannot do
these things nowadays; the *Conzertstück* puts all later and more
ambitious efforts to shame. Once upon a time it was thought to
be great music. When that delusion was dispelled, we proceeded
to mistake it for bad music. This was a worse, because a snobbish,
delusion. Weber, in all his innocence, has far more kinship with
Beethoven than with his fellow-pupil Meyerbeer; and the nearest
classical parallel to the mood, as well as the 'programme', of his
finale is the finale of Beethoven's *Lebewohl* Sonata. The art of
'registering' emotions is no mean accomplishment, whether it be
achieved at Hollywood in 1931 or at Dresden in 1821. And in that
art Weber never fumbles. He may move awkwardly from one
situation to the next; the stage carpenter may even appear in
shirt-sleeves during the transformation-scenes; but the emotions
are unmistakable and commanding of respect. One exception must
be admitted, though it is not evident in the *Conzertstück*. Weber
died young, and his style had not yet become always equal to

expressing joy; in moments of jubilation his characters sometimes
seem to borrow their rhythms from the poultry-yard. But the finale
of the *Conzertstück* does not deserve any such charge. We must
go to Beethoven for any deeper glow of joy; and Weber does not
here expose himself to any damaging comparison, for he attempts
no form on a scale that he cannot perfectly master. The four
movements are astonishingly successful in covering the exact
ground of their own ideas at such length as leaves each ready to
lead to the next. The way in which the end (or rather the debouch-
ing) of the Larghetto anticipates the theme of the Allegro (Ex. 2)
is as ingenious as any device of Liszt. A few weeping notes of a
solitary bassoon indicate the Châtelaine's return to consciousness
before the march is heard. These notes are a *locus classicus* for
the perfect dramatic use of a special quality of tone. The march
itself has a sentimental touch in all its phrases (see the cadence
into the fourth bar) that exactly fits the romantic situation. A
real march would never do: we want a tapestry march for our
tapestry châtelaine. On the modern pianoforte, octave glissandos,
especially when upward, are rasping to the finger-nails. But they
make admirable screams. As to the finale, I frankly confess that
it thrills me. Weber's range of harmony is hardly wider than
Gluck's; and when he gets beyond tonic and dominant his changes
are really as grand in effect as in intention. As for the pianoforte
writing, it conclusively proves Weber to have deserved his reputation as one of the greatest players ever known on any instrument.
Every detail of it must have been discovered during extemporization
at full speed: there is no other means of guessing that such passages
lie well for the hand at all. And yet there are people who try to
modernize Weber's pianoforte style! We might as well psycho-
analyse his Châtelaine.

CLVII. A SCHUBERT CENTENARY CONCERT, 1928

Why commemorate Schubert in an orchestral programme consisting mainly of arrangements? Those who know most about
Schubert's orchestral and operatic works will be least surprised
at this procedure. Schubert's mature symphonic style is represented by one and a half symphonies. These require no centenary
occasion to bring them to a hearing. If we explore the other
symphonies of Schubert we must be prepared for a kind of stiff
Mozartean style, charming in itself and frequently foreshadowing
the great Schubert in passages mostly pretty and quaint, but
occasionally suggestive of deeper thoughts. Yet suggestions and
foreshadowings are all that we shall get, and we shall fail to represent Schubert's mature orchestral ideas. Must we, then, be content

to add to the innumerable performances of the famous one and a half symphonies, or is there some other way in which we can reveal new aspects of the Schubertean orchestra?

Those who have studied Schubert's operas and his vast body of four-hand pianoforte music know that in these repositories a world of magnificent orchestral art lies buried; buried in the operas beneath hopelessly undramatic libretti; buried in the four-hand music for mere lack of opportunity for the composer to produce it in orchestral form. Who, for instance, can suppose that a piece entitled 'Funeral March for the Czar' was intended to exist only in a four-hand pianoforte version? All four-hand pianoforte music tends to sound orchestral, if only because of its full and widely spaced harmony. Perhaps Mozart's glorious four-hand Sonata in F is the only duet that does not constantly suggest orchestral possibilities, and even then I find myself longing to hear it as a string quintet. In any case the orchestration, in a decent classical style, of Schubert's four-hand music could do no harm even if the originals were known to the public. But who, as a matter of fact, has ever heard Schubert's four-hand music once in ten years, either in public or in private? And, among amateurs who cultivate four-hand playing, how many really know what works are original and what are arrangements? Most people nowadays know that Haydn did not write his symphonies for pianoforte duet; but it is possible that popular opinion has gone to the other extreme, and does not believe in the existence of any original four-hand works. If some of the arrangements produced in the present programme have the effect of inciting pianists to hunt in couples after the originals, purists will be compelled in their own interests to condone our experiments.

The fate of Schubert's operatic music is tragic. From the much maligned (but by Schubert and Beethoven almost as much beloved) Salieri, Schubert learnt a good Italian diction for *opera buffa*, and, incidentally, for *opera seria*. But he did not learn two things: first, to know when a text or a situation was hopelessly undramatic, and secondly, the duty and art of bullying his librettist until the text became dramatic. Comic dialogue and ensemble he learnt, doubtless with real help from Salieri, to handle deftly enough; and the pieces in his operas which depend on this skill are in a style thoroughly Schubertean, but hardly to be found anywhere else in his works; certainly not in his songs, which are at the opposite pole from opera. And that is where the trouble began. Schubert soon left the region of *opera buffa* and developed a healthy appetite for blood-and-thunder libretti which his remarkably incompetent friends supplied with deadly facility. The story of his operatic ventures is depressing, and space does not admit of more detail here. The conclusion of the whole matter at the present day is that when, at the instigation of Fritz Busch, I entered into a scheme for rescuing some of the best music in Schubert's operas by expanding existing libretti so as to include movements from works that could not be saved as wholes, the distinguished dramatist Rolf Lauckner (with whom I also produced a new version of *Euryanthe*) was able to find only two libretti that could by any process be got into tolerable shape. These were, a pretty little work, *Der treue Soldat* (alias *Der vierjährige Posten*), written by Schubert at the age of seventeen, and full of his most amiable Mozartishness; and a quite witty comedy by a writer of some reputation, Castelli, originally entitled *Der Häusliche Krieg*, and now renamed *Die Weiberverschwörung*. *The Faithful Sentinel* was produced in London, not long before the centenary, at the Court Theatre, London, and, Lord! how it infuriated the critics! We know so much about opera in these British Isles that any departure from its most obvious rules and customs must be visited with the wrath due to a breach of etiquette at a tea-party of washer-women, though the composer died a hundred years ago and was only seventeen at the time of the indiscretion. Meantime that vile pot-pourri *Drei-Mäder-Haus*, or *Lilac Time*, continues to draw full houses, and is regarded in this country as a thing in which a self-respecting artist can appear.

CLVIII. *a*. OVERTURE, DIE 'WEIBERVERSCHWÖRUNG'
(THE CONSPIRACY OF WIVES)

To *Der Häusliche Krieg* (Domestic Warfare) Schubert wrote no overture. In adapting this opera to a revised version of its libretto the object we (that is to say Fritz Busch, the poet Rolf Lauckner, and the present writer) had in mind was twofold, being not only to make the opera presentable as regards its original contents but also to provide in it a suitable environment for as many other beautiful pieces from Schubert's operas and fragments as possible. The reconstructed *Weiberverschwörung* and the early *Treuer Soldat* have thus, between them, brought nearly a dozen pieces of Schubert's best music, in a wide range of style, into an environment where they can be enjoyed. It is not too much to say that hitherto not only these pieces but the two operas as wholes and as collections of music have been quite inaccessible to the public.

The first requirement of *Die Weiberverschwörung* was, then, an overture. The opera is comic, with the comedy of manners.

A comic overture, then, was needed; and one not too remote in period was at hand in the shape of the delightful overture to *Die Zwillingsbruder* (The Twin Brothers), a one-act farce which was actually produced, but with so little self-confidence on Schubert's part that he did not even sit through the performance, though he did not go so far as Charles Lamb, who led the chorus that hissed his own piece off the stage. But the overture was a decided success, though the rest was ruined by the libretto. Now comedy is not quite enough for *Die Weiberverschwörung*. The comic element is heightened by the all-pervading atmosphere of medieval chivalry. The conspiring wives are the grass-widows of Crusaders, and their conspiracy is an agreement to compel their husbands to stay at home in future by refusing to show them any affection until they have sworn never to go to war again. A page-boy of the chief of the Crusaders has hurried home in front of them, and, while pursuing his own love affairs, has attended the meeting of the conspirators, disguised as a woman. He hastens back to the Crusaders and betrays the plot. So they puzzle their wives by ostentatious coldness on their own part. Eventually the page, with a great show of divulging a mystery, tells the ladies that the men, finding themselves in great danger in the East, had solemnly vowed that if Heaven would bring them safe home again they would take their wives with them as additional warriors on their next crusade. The wives thereupon make a dash for the armoury and put up with such misfits as come their way. And it still takes some time for the comedy to unravel.

No music can be too light-hearted for all this. But some hint of chivalric pomp must be given. And here Schubert has kindly provided us with an ideally fitting introduction to this overture. Among the four-hand pieces there is an overture in F with an introduction in F minor. The rest of the overture is an unattractive example of Schubert's worst Italian manner, but the introduction is first-rate, quaintly pompous, intensely Schubertean, and, by a final miracle, requires a change of only one note to make one of its themes anticipate that of the overture to *Die Zwillingsbruder*. Into D minor, then, this introduction shall go; and here, in the following four examples, you have the main themes of the resulting overture to *Die Weiberverschwörung*. The introduction also proved supremely useful in a difficult piece of musical carpentry later in the opera.

Ex. 1.

Largo.

Ex. 2.

Original.

Ex. 3.

Ex. 4.

b. POLONAISE IN F MAJOR

This orchestration of one of Schubert's four-hand Polonaises is used in *Die Weiberverschwörung* to bring up the curtain upon the scene of the Crusaders resting in their camp a few hours' march from home.

c.

At this point in my Schubert Centenary Concert we played Joachim's version of the Grand Duo as a Symphony. This is described in vol. i, pp. 215–18. I take the opportunity of inserting here an account of the overture to the other Schubert opera, which we played at a later concert.

CLIX. OVERTURE TO 'THE FAITHFUL SENTINEL'

Der Vierjähriger Posten is a one-act opera which Schubert wrote, in the same year as his wonderful Mass in F, at the age of sixteen.

The plot is simple. A regiment that was quartered in a certain village received marching orders so suddenly that our hero was overlooked. He awoke to find his regiment gone, and, having no explanation of their disappearance, proceeded to make love to the heroine, a sweet maiden of the village. The curtain rises upon the day when, after four years of idyllic life, the lovers are confronted with the prospect of the immediate return of the hero's regiment. Death awaits the 'deserter'; but he has the happy idea of putting on his uniform and showing himself to his regiment as still on the sentry-go from which he has not been relieved for four years.

The dramatist Rolf Lauckner, who has worked with me and Fritz Busch in the rehabilitation of this and of another Schubert opera, and of Weber's *Euryanthe*, has added another character, the châtelaine whom the faithful sentinel has to guard. By this means we have been able to rescue several beautiful pieces from Schubert's other operas, and to give the slender plot a backbone, or at least a rib.

These changes do not affect the overture, which shows Schubert's genius in charming boyishness. To prune its obvious redundancies would be sillier than any of the obvious defects that result from the boy's manifest delight and excitement over his own ideas. Stevenson's tadpole was quite right in laughing at the frog who scolded him for having a tail. The frog was wrong in denying that he himself had had a tail as a tadpole; and the tadpole was mistaken in inferring that the frog had never been a tadpole.

This Schubertean tadpole begins with an intelligent anticipation of one of the subtlest and ripest of Schubert's later songs, the *Pause* in *Die Schöne Müllerin*.

Ex. 1.

Its purport is the profound calm of the country-side and country folk. A modulation to B flat strikes a darker note, without leaving the mood of picturesqueness.

The allegro starts with a delicious tune which the boy-composer cannot hear too often.

Ex. 2.

Slight alterations will suffice (as with Haydn) to make it pass for a new theme; and even the really different 'second subject' would, on the other hand, do perfectly well for a mere second strain to it; though it takes the form of a two-part round.

Ex. 3.

There are other ideas, mainly cadential; but here you have all the important matter of the overture. The modulations are masterly, and show a natural sense of the theatre as well as of pure music.

CLX. ENTR'ACTE IN B MINOR AND BALLET IN G MAJOR, FROM 'ROSAMUNDE'. MARCH IN E MAJOR

Rosamunde is not an opera, but a play to which Schubert wrote incidental music consisting of an overture, three entr'actes, two ballets, a song, a chorus of ghosts or spirits, a chorus of shepherds, a chorus of huntsmen, and a pastoral melody. The heroine was not Fair Rosamond, but the Queen of Cyprus. Further checks to our curiosity are that the authoress was the gifted Helmine von Chezy who made such an unholy mess of Weber's *Euryanthe*, and that this particular play is lost. Which is just as well. If anything she wrote could have had an illuminating relation to such grand tragic music as Schubert's B minor Entr'acte, she would have been a great poet. And we know that she was not.

To my surprise I had some difficulty in obtaining parts of the B minor Entr'acte. It seems to have dropped out of recent orchestral repertoires. *Rosamunde* is now represented mainly by the Overture to *Die Zauberharfe*, while its real overture, a much slighter effort, has been assigned to the opera *Alphonso und Estrella*; and the rest of the music is represented only by the lighter ballets. And even these have been re-orchestrated by Reger, whose untimely death makes it impossible to ask him why.

The B minor Entr'acte, with its rhythms which at first seem stiff, but which accumulate to massiveness, was at one time a hackneyed piece. Its opening theme—

Ex. 1.

soon develops the characteristic Schubert-Rossini pathos of a soft change to the major mode. Later, a lamenting theme appears in the dominant—

Ex. 2.

and is followed by a solemn passage which every British musician among my contemporaries will remember to have been quoted with due reverence in Prout's treatises on instrumentation.

Ex. 3.

The delicious Ballet in G requires neither quotation nor comment.

The March in E is one of the most brilliant of Schubert's four-hand pieces; and though it is delightful to play on the pianoforte, every note of it cries for orchestration. In *Die Weiberverschwörung* it is obviously ideally suited to the moment when the ladies rush to the armoury to equip themselves; and the trio underlines the feminine element deliciously.

CLXI. FANTASIA ('THE WANDERER'), ARRANGED FOR PIANOFORTE AND ORCHESTRA BY LISZT

The 'Wanderer' Fantasia had a special interest for Liszt, because, without any revolutionary gestures, it solved the problem of the 'Symphonic Poem', that new art-form by which Liszt was trying to achieve for instrumental music what Wagner, quite independently, was achieving in opera; that is to say, a music that can fill an hour without breaking up into self-contained smaller designs. For this purpose certain new ways of developing and connecting themes were needed, and Schubert provided them in full maturity in this unique composition. Not only is the Wagner-Liszt leit-motiv system present, but there is also the far more important and difficult achievement of transforming whole sections into new rhythmic and characteristic forms. Perhaps the cleverest thing in all Liszt's works is the scherzo of his Faust Symphony. In the character of Mephistopheles that scherzo parodies the whole first movement, which was a tragic and dignified portrait of Faust. Schubert, with none but the most amiable thoughts, provides the whole technical and aesthetic method of such transformations in what may be called the scherzo of the 'Wanderer' Fantasia.

Another point which interested Liszt in this work is the reason which induced him to arrange it for orchestra with pianoforte. It is thoroughly orchestral in conception, and, like the Grand Duo which Joachim has been said to have 'restored to its rightful dignity as a symphony', often shows up the incapacity of the pianoforte to give the true orchestral 'punch' to the climaxes. It is defensible, as Schubert himself abundantly shows, to write orchestrally for the pianoforte and the string quartet, in the sense that the writing suggests orchestral qualities; but that is quite another story. Schubert was not a great pianist, and he might have written more scrupulously for the pianoforte if he had been unable to play it at all. As it was, he played like a bold score-reader, and broke off in the middle of the finale of the 'Wanderer' Fantasia, saying, 'The devil may play it!'

So this is where Liszt comes in, not as a Vandal showman, but as a pious exponent of Schubert's meaning. Sometimes the virtuoso gets the better of the exponent, and Liszt cannot resist a mild attack of glass-chandelier pianistics. These lapses create an impression out of all proportion to their actual wickedness; but nothing is easier than to correct them. We have only to restore Schubert's original figures, not too literally, but adapted to their orchestral surroundings. Purists have much to learn if they condemn this work of Liszt, thus corrected, on general grounds of piety. From such critics one might fear a double charge of impiety, to Liszt as well as to Schubert!

I now give a short analysis of the 'Wanderer' Fantasia, based on the original text without reference to Liszt's arrangement. The possibility of so doing proves the faithfulness of Liszt's work; and the audience will be all the better able to appreciate the ingenuity and insight with which the material has been divided between the pianoforte and the orchestra. As for the orchestration, it is hard to see where the purist can cavil; certainly not on grounds of display or noisiness. Liszt's brass is not quite classical, but neither is Schubert's, as Brahms proved when he prevented Joachim from imitating it in the orchestration of the Grand Duo. And no praise can be too high for the acumen with which Liszt has left the thundering opening of the fugal finale just as Schubert wrote it, for the pianoforte alone. It is extremely difficult to stamp out the widespread heresy that orchestral basses, even with all Wagner's tubas and all Paderewski's sarrusophones, can either roar like organ-pedals or bang like the bottom octave of the pianoforte.

Schubert begins with a broad symphonic formula, the rhythmic figure of which pervades the whole work in Beethovenish style. To save space I give, underneath my sketch of this opening, the form afterwards given to it in the scherzo.

Ex. 1:

Deliberately and clearly the movement drifts away from the course suggested by its sonata-like opening; and one of its most remarkable qualities is its complete certainty in its own business. It shows no sign of hovering between two inconsistent hypotheses, as in some cases where Schubert has begun a dramatic movement with a merely lyric idea. From the outset the 'Wanderer' Fantasia belies its title. As Wagner's Hans Sachs says of Walther's singing,

'Though he deserted our guide-rails, his step was firm and unerring'. For such freedom in the alternation of stormy developments with quiet quasi-lyric passages, and such leisurely breadth in the approach to climaxes, we must return to the concertos of Bach (which Schubert did not know); and for such perfect handling of the remotest possible key-relations we must look forward to Wagner.

Of the two quiet episodes in this energetic movement the first is in E major, on the rhythmic figure of the opening—

Ex. 2.

and the second, in E flat, reappears later, transformed as a kind of trio to the scherzo.

Ex. 3.

FIRST MOVEMENT.

SCHERZO.

The development that follows Ex. 3 is very extensive and modulates to the immensely remote region of C sharp minor, on the dominant of which an impressive diminuendo leads to the slow movement in that key. This is a kind of set of variations on the central tune of one of Schubert's greatest songs, *Der Wanderer*; hence the title (not Schubert's) by which the work is known. I say 'a kind of set of variations' because the variations all arise as so many continuations of a tune that has no end. Here again, we find Schubert devising a unique form which solves another difficulty in the Wagner-Liszt problem of a music more continuous than that of sonatas.

Here is the beginning of the 'Wanderer' tune, which, like all the rest of the Fantasia, seems to arise from the rhythmic figure of Ex. 1.

Ex. 4.

The later continuations (or variations) rise to a stormy climax, which undoubtedly gains much by being shared with an orchestra. The descent from this modulates to E major, and dies away in

distant thunder. The last reverberations of this thunder suddenly
become the opening figure of a scherzo in A flat.

Ex. 5.

The continuation is indicated in the lower stave of Ex. 1. Schubert
carries the transformation far enough to show that nothing need
have prevented him from anticipating Liszt's Faust Symphony
to the extent of thus paraphrasing the whole movement. Yet he
does not choose thus to restrict himself, but allows other new
ideas to arise from his material; such as this irresistible little waltz—

Ex. 6.

At length he starts what sounds like a trio. But this, as we have
seen in Ex. 3, is a transformation of the second episode in the
first movement. And here, too, it is not allowed to become more
than an episode. Soon the main theme returns, but only to
modulate widely and angrily. Schubert and the modern player
can again be grateful to Liszt and to his orchestra for here sub-
stituting passages which others than the devil may play. This
storm leads to the finale, a thundering fugue, the simple-seeming
grotesque counterpoint of which the British Doctor of Music
will be well advised to regard with respect. Here is its subject:

Ex. 7.

In its later developments the need for an orchestra is very evident,
and Liszt's work would amply justify its existence by the mere
achievement of making this finale attain a sonorous and effortless
climax.

BERLIOZ

CLXII. 'HAROLD IN ITALY', SYMPHONY WITH VIOLA OBBLIGATO, OP. 16

1. *Harold in the Mountains. Scenes of melancholy, happiness, and joy.*
2. *March of Pilgrims singing their evening prayer.*
3. *Serenade of a mountain-dweller in the Abbruzzi to his mistress.*
4. *Orgy of Brigands. Memories of past scenes.*

There are excellent reasons for reading *Childe Harold's Pilgrimage*. But among them I cannot find any that concern Berlioz and this symphony, except for the jejune value of the discovery that no definite elements of Byron's poem have penetrated the impregnable fortress of Berlioz's encyclopaedic inattention. Many picturesque things are described in famous stanzas in *Childe Harold*; but nothing remotely resembling Berlioz's Pilgrims' March, nor his serenade in the Abbruzzi. As to the brigands, Byron has described the varieties of costume in a crowd of mixed nationality consisting undoubtedly of potential brigands; but the passage is not in the Italian cantos, and Berlioz tells us that his work concerns Harold in Italy. On the other hand there is no trace in Berlioz's music of any of the famous passages in *Childe Harold*. No doubt 'there was a sound of revelry by night' in the Orgy of Brigands, but the Duchess of Richmond's ball was not an orgy of brigands, nor was it interrupted by a march of pilgrims singing their evening prayer. Nor is there anything to correspond to an invocation of the ocean, except a multitude of grammatical solecisms equivalent to Byron's 'there let him lay'.

There, then, let Berlioz lie; the whitest liar since Cyrano de Bergerac. (This sentence is a completely Berliozian enharmonic modulation.) There is a river in Monmouth and a river in Macedon; there is a B in Byron and a B in Berlioz; and as Byron stood upon the Bridge of Sighs and stood in the Coliseum, and in this and that historic or picturesque spot, to meditate on history, politics, and family affairs, so the viola solo delivers its *idée fixe* unchanged and unadorned, while Berlioz does whatever occurs to him to do with his orchestra. There is nothing Byronic about that *idée fixe*. It did not occur to him in connexion with Byron. It comes in fully ripe glory of instrumentation, exactly as in the *Harold* Symphony, except that it is for a cor anglais an octave higher than its position in the viola, in a work described by Berlioz as an early indiscretion which he burnt, an overture to *Rob Roy*. In Berlioz's vocabulary 'burnt' means carefully preserved, so that an admiring posterity can discover evidence of the truth of Oscar Wilde's assertion that a true artist lives in a series of masterpieces in which no progress whatever can be discerned. The Overture to

Rob Roy turned up early in this century, and proved to be quite a presentable and engaging work. Mendelssohn declared that what he found so Philistine about Berlioz was that 'with all his efforts to go stark mad he never once succeeds'. From its own standpoint the criticism was neither unfriendly nor untrue; a large part of Berlioz's charm consists in his earnest aspirations to achieve the glamour of a desperate wickedness against the background of his inveterate and easily shockable respectability. Poor Byron had Lady Byron for his background. Berlioz had to content himself with his master Cherubini. Master and pupil deserved each other: you have only to read Cherubini's treatise on counterpoint to see the psychological origin of all revolutions; and you have only to read Berlioz's own account of his diplomatic triumphs over Cherubini to see how low human nature can sink, when an ill-bred younger artist gets his chance of scoring off a disappointed old one.

On the whole, Berlioz's imaginary wickednesses are more amiable than the virtues, real or imaginary, for which he professes admiration. He is as adventurous as Jules Verne, who never went farther from his native Amiens than Paris, and spoke no language but French, though he sent Mr. Phileas Fogg of the London Reform Club round the world in eighty days, and a small company of Franco-Algerians, Russians, and other nationalities round the solar system on a fragment of a comet in eighteen months. And Berlioz is quite as innocent as Jules Verne, though he also succeeds when he is as macabre as Poe. Perhaps only the profounder Verne-scholars are aware that Jules Verne also made an essay in the macabre, in his story of Maître Zacharius the clockmaker, whose soul went into his clocks and watches, until it came to a bad end in his masterpiece which, designed to display pious texts every hour, suddenly took to displaying horrid blasphemies, till at midnight it burst with a thunderclap, while the soul of its author went Elsewhere. There are some quite good Berliozian touches in the Verneal innocence, and I am strongly inclined to trace the resemblances between Harold in Italy and Hector Servadac on the comet Gallia.

But—and this is a very big but—Berlioz, whose genius for instrumentation has always been acknowledged, also had a genius for composition. Two causes have prevented the recognition of this: first, that he notoriously failed to learn anything his masters tried to teach him; and, secondly, that almost everything they tried to teach him was wrong. The musical authorities of Paris in the first quarter of the nineteenth century had been the Latin contemporaries of the supreme Viennese classics of instrumental music. These classics were as foreign to them as Berlioz's adored Shakespeare (with or without *la dénouement de Garrick*); yet the Parisian ideas of musical form were supposed to have advanced with the times; and Berlioz undoubtedly thought that the expositions of the first allegros in his *Fantastique* and *Harold* Symphonies were symphonic expositions in the style established by Mozart and Haydn and developed by Beethoven. To us such an idea seems ridiculous; it is like constructing the first act of a drama round the incident of the loss of an umbrella which turns out to have no connexion with the plot; and we naturally blame Berlioz for so obviously deficient a sense of form. But, in the first place, did his teachers know better? Cherubini had a very good sense of form; he was profoundly moved by Haydn and Mozart, nor did Beethoven fail to influence him more than he liked to admit to himself. But his treatment of the Viennese forms results only by a precarious series of flukes in anything that can be judged by the same criteria; and in some of his best movements, such as the overture to *Anacreon*, the form has no resemblance to that of any other classic, ancient or contemporary. We had better ascertain what Cherubini thought about form before we decide whether Berlioz thought likewise, otherwise, rightly, or wrongly. In the second place, we shall be driven to recognize that his genius for composition is independent of any external shapes. His sonata expositions are quite flat and do not establish their 'complementary key'. Then why call them sonata expositions? They are very clear, entertaining, and all the better for the repeats which Berlioz prescribes. He cannot 'develop' a theme; he can only submit it to a process aptly described by Dannreuther as 'rabbeting'. But this process leads to excellent climaxes, whatever it may be called. And what about Berlioz's codas? Ah, there his natural element coincides with the classical form; he is a born perorator, and everything leads up to his perorations. But notice that everything does genuinely lead up to them; he does not perorate upon a vacuum. He cannot argue; he cannot meditate: he has at least this in common with Byron that 'sobald er reflektirt ist er ein Kind'. But he can sum up and pile on the agony or the exultation; he can also begin at a real beginning. I am not quite certain about his middle. Just as his harmony is, like even his divinest instrumentation, all top and bottom, so there is a certain hollowness about his forms, apart from the fact that they are in any case totally different from (and infinitely better than) anything they profess to be. From the two typical defects of bad highbrow music Berlioz is absolutely free: he never writes a piece consisting of introductions to introductions; and he never writes a piece consisting, like the Intermezzo (and most of the rest) of *Cavalleria*, entirely of impassioned ends. His hollowness may be said, in Hibernian metaphor, to lie on the surface; inwardly all is as true as if Mr. Gulliver had spoken it.

Perhaps the most gloriously nonsensical fact about the *Harold*

Symphony is that its viola solo is the result of the work having been commissioned by Paganini, who is said to have played it at the first performance in 1834.[1] Anything less like a concerto has never been conceived: the part has its difficulties of endurance, tone-production, and conception, but is about as suited for the display of a virtuoso's powers as a bath-chair for a world's speed-record.

You have now (if I have had the honour of your undivided attention thus far) read as close an analysis of the 'programme' of the *Harold* Symphony as the tangential velocity of Berlioz's mind permits the sympathetic analyst to achieve; and all that remains is to quote the themes.

I. *Harold aux Montagnes.*

Introduction.—A melancholy double fugue or round, typical of Berlioz's broadest openings, arises from the depths (Exx. 1 and 2)—

Ex. 1.

Ex. 2.

and leads to a minor version, announced by the wood-wind, of the main theme (Rob-Roy-Servadac-Harold-Byron-Berlioz), which soon afterwards enters more dramatically in the major on Paganini's viola.

Ex. 3.

BERLIOZ.

BEETHOVEN.

[1] Both Berlioz and Paganini drew the line somewhere. Paganini refused to play the work but persisted in paying for it.

This entry is admirably timed. The theme is accompanied by a harp and two clarinets in thirds. From Berlioz's treatise on instrumentation we learn that, in the language of Hollywood, soft cantabile clarinets in thirds 'register' chastity; and, thanks to Berlioz, the works of Marie Antoinette's favourite composer Sacchini now survive for us solely in a couple of such thirds with which that master accompanied the downcasting of Eriphyle's eyes on receiving a proposal. Thus surrounded by the virtue which sultans revere so highly as to delegate it to their potential or actual wives, Harold surveys the scene. His delightful theme, after a meditative continuation harmonized in the style of 'there let him lay', is soon restated in a most gorgeous orchestration in which the winds echo the strings at the distance of one beat. I have purposely quoted almost the whole theme, and shall quote equally largely from others, to bring out the fact, insufficiently appreciated even by some who have glorified Berlioz at the expense of Beethoven, that Berlioz is eminently a master of the long melodic paragraph. The resemblance of this tune to the main theme of the Vivace of Beethoven's Seventh Symphony has often been noted, and it is a very curious and by no means superficial fact. The two themes are related as widely contrasted variations of the same idea, and the resemblance covers the whole first eight bars.

After the glorious restatement has died away, an allegro begins with a group of lively figures upon which Harold-Rob-Roy-Hector-&c., intervenes with palpitations that lead to a crisis in the full orchestra. Then the viola, after spelling out the first five notes gradually, announces the following cheerful melody:

Ex. 4.

Allegro.

Restatements of this in dialogue with the full orchestra are suddenly interrupted by a new theme in an unexpected key.

Ex. 5.

Proceeding conversationally from thence to D major, where it is developed and echoed by the wind with displaced rhythm, this does duty for the second group of what Berlioz undoubtedly took for a sonata exposition. He accordingly repeats the whole from Ex. 4, and then proceeds to a development leading to a free recapitulation that gradually merges into a coda at least twice the length of all the rest of the movement. It flows magnificently, and reintroduces Harold himself in a kind of fugue, started very impressively by the double basses and taken up in gradually quicker vibration by the other parts.

II. *Marche de Pèlerins.*

After some mysterious chords the song of the approaching pilgrims is heard.

Ex. 6.

It is punctuated by muttered prayers—

Ex. 7.

which are accompanied by the sounds of two bells that impart strange modulations to the harmony at every phrase.

After four phrases on the lines of Ex. 6, the melody descends to the bass, and Harold, with his slow theme, contemplates the approaching pilgrims. They continue to approach for no less than twelve phrases in all. Then a more solemn hymn (canto religioso) is heard high in the air—

Ex. 8.

Wind.

Strings.

while the footsteps of the pilgrims retreat in unbroken march, represented by pizzicato basses. The viola accompanies with mysteriously rustling arpeggios, *sul ponticello*, no longer representing Harold, but some angelic or natural phenomenon. The first theme, Ex. 6, returns in its own E major, punctuated by Ex. 7. At last the bell-notes of Ex. 7 and the retreating footsteps are almost all that is heard in a die-away of fantastic length and originality.

III. *Sérénade d'un Montagnard des Abruzzi.*

After some lively pipings over a drone-bass—

Ex. 9.

Allegro assai.

3 times.   twice.

&c.

a cor anglais begins the vocal substance of the serenade in a tempo twice as slow.

Ex. 10.

Allegretto.

Soon Harold appears and contemplates the scene benignantly, while the serenade proceeds independently. His sympathies are roused to more lively utterance as the vocal serenade reaches its end. Then the introductory pipings are resumed. Their lively rhythm is then combined with the slower rhythm of the serenade, now played by the viola, while the Harold theme hovers in bell-like tones (harp-harmonics and flute) above, until all dies away.

IV. *Orgie de Brigands. Souvenirs de scènes précédentes.*

Beethoven, in the introduction to the choral part of his Ninth Symphony, may have suggested to Berlioz the notion of the *souvenirs de scènes précédentes*; but Berlioz's execution of this

design is his own. With admirable sense he begins at once,
allegro frenetico, with his brigands, stating their theme shortly.
It 'registers' franticness and frightfulness in the cross-rhythms of
its last four bars.

Ex. 11.

The memory of the melancholy part of the introduction (Exx. 1
and 2) arises. 'We'll none of that!' say the brigands. The pilgrims'
march (Ex. 6) rouses a less immediate but more uneasy opposition.
The serenade (Ex. 10) is fiercely suppressed; but the memory of
Harold's own past happiness (Allegro, Ex. 4) is not so easily
ousted. And, whatever may have induced Harold to enrol himself
among the brigands, it is a moment of genuine pathos as well as
of genuine music when he parts with his very identity in the last
broken reminiscences of the main theme (Ex. 3), now heard faintly
in those chaste clarinets, echoed with sobs, and dying away slowly
at the beginning of its fourth bar. Sardonic laughter is heard,
growing to exultant cries; and the orgy starts in full vigour. You
will learn most about Berlioz's brigands from *Lélio*, his sequel to
the *Symphonie Fantastique*. According to *Lélio* they are, in their
boisterous way, very gallant to ladies—

Ex. 12.

whom they invite to drink from cups made of the skulls of their
lovers. The following passage may possibly show how the raw
material of these utensils is obtained; at all events it is eminently
suggestive of bright deaths quivering at victims' throats, of streams
of gore, and of round objects rolling on the ground.

Ex. 13.

con gravita.

IV   G

Pathetic pleas for mercy are also heard—

Ex. 14.

and are received, we regret to say, with fiendish laughter.

Ex. 15.

Berlioz traverses this mass of material twice. Then a very short passage of development leads to the beginning of a recapitulation of Ex. 12 in the tonic major. Suddenly it is interrupted. With palpitating heart Harold listens to the chant of the pilgrims; no mere reminiscence this time, but the real sound in the distance. This breaks his heart; he can endure life no longer; he drinks poison and leaves the brigands to finish their orgy without him.

CLXIII. OVERTURE TO 'KING LEAR'

One of the largest and most curious subjects in musical aesthetics is the capacity of music to illustrate things outside music. The most difficult question in this subject is the capacity of the composer to attend to the thing he purports to illustrate. In the case of Berlioz the problem is simple; for his capacity for attending to anything but the most immediate melodic, orchestral, and rhetorical impulses is nil; and as for accepting his own statements about anything in his life or his works, you would be far wiser to hang a dog on the evidence of Benvenuto Cellini (Berlioz's own ideal), supported by Captain Lemuel Gulliver and Cyrano de Bergerac. In one way, and one only, Berlioz was perfectly truthful; he is a noble example of aesthetic sincerity. What he tells us of his enthusiasms and hatreds may be taken as the bare truth without exaggeration or softening. Every other statement that he makes should be regarded as possibly an unscrupulous invention in support of his prejudices. He saw no harm in saying that at the first performance of his *Grande Messe des Morts* he averted disaster by taking up the baton when Habeneck laid it down at a critical moment to take a pinch of snuff. Many years after this story had made Habeneck infamous throughout Europe, Berlioz coolly confessed that he had told it simply because it was *ben trovato*. Probably there is just as much truth in the wonderful tale of passion which he tells us was the origin of his *King Lear*

Overture. According to that tale the inspiration came during or after a crisis of jealousy in one of his love-affairs, when he rushed off on a journey with the purpose of murdering his beloved. According to the title of the work, you ought to read Shakespeare's *King Lear* to find out the meaning of the music. But no one who has any independent power of following Shakespeare as drama and Berlioz as music will waste five minutes over the attempt to connect Berlioz's *King Lear* with Shakespeare's. He may go so far as to agree with Richard Strauss that the startling shrill pizzicato chord at the chief climax of the work suggests something snapping in the mad king's brain; but that detail is not to be found in Shakespeare, nor has Berlioz left that (or any) explanation of it. Again, nobody need quarrel with the suggestion that the beautiful melody for the oboe in the introduction is worthy of Cordelia; but it is quite another question whether, if Cordelia could ever have expressed herself so freely and attractively, the tragedy would have happened at all. Again, what elements or persons in the play are we to connect with the second subject of the allegro (Ex. 3 and its continuations)? Surely not Cordelia; if the melody in the introduction might perhaps claim to sound the depths of Cordelia's heart and show us the tenderness her father could not find in her sincerity, *this* kind of melody wears its heart on its sleeve. And no one who knows Berlioz's ideas of the beautiful will dare to suggest that these themes are meant to show the specious 'tender-hefted nature' of Regan or Goneril; though it would on that theory be easy to explain the furious transformation of Ex. 3 (just before 'something snaps', according to Richard Strauss's interpretation) as the unmasking of their true character. Berlioz, however, we may be sure, intended these melodies to be types of pure beauty. There is no other feminine element in the play, and I would like to see the faces of Kent and Edgar if they were confronted with Ex. 3 and its continuation as the expression of their devotion and sympathy. Even in externals, such as Berlioz most enjoyed to handle realistically, you will not be able to fit this work to *King Lear*. Where are the thunderstorms? The drum-figure ♪♪♪♪ ♩ in the introduction is very impressive; but it is everything else that thunder is not: it is rhythmic, it ends with a crack which does not reverberate, and it is invariable. Berlioz never meant it for thunder: when he wants thunder he can get it with highly poetic and accurate observation of the facts, as in his *Scène aux Champs*.

In short, we shall only misunderstand Berlioz's *King Lear* Overture so long as we try to connect it with Shakespeare's Lear at all.

What Berlioz has achieved is exactly what he has attempted: a magnificent piece of orchestral rhetoric in tragic style, inspired neither by particular passages in literature nor by particular events in Berlioz's life, but by much the same impulses that lead him to tell effective tales of himself, of his friends, and of enemies, whether under the guise of memoirs or of the brilliant and witty fiction of his *Soirées d'orchestre*. Above all, he is inspired by the orchestra itself. You have only to dip into his *Traité d'Instrumentation* to see that even as a prose-writer (in which capacity he is more adroit than as a musician) the mere tone of an orchestral instrument inspires him, much as Nature inspires Ruskin, with vivid powers of description and characterization. Indeed, Ruskin and Berlioz have enough in common to make an imaginary conversation between them full of comic possibilities: Ruskin would disapprove horrifically of all Berlioz's tastes and artistic methods; and yet the two men have the same burning proselytizing sincerity and the same lack of suspicion that a wider knowledge might change their opinion of much that was distasteful to them at the moment. The oddest part of it is that Berlioz, whose sublimest music is constantly at the mercy of a total lack of sense of the ridiculous, is full of humour as a prose-writer, and would make glorious fun of Ruskin in our imaginary conversation, which, if properly conducted, ought to leave them excellent friends cheerfully convinced of each other's perdition. This one point, that Berlioz is a master of humour in prose and notoriously without sense of humour in music, ought to convince us of the hopelessness of looking to external subject-matter as a guide to music, even where the music is given an external title by the composer. If the music does achieve a real connexion, it will illustrate the subject; but you will get nothing out of the expectation that the subject will illustrate it. The music can express moods, just as nature can inspire moods. And sometimes these moods may fit certain dramatic situations, so that nature or music may seem to sympathize. Not less often the artist uses the power of nature or music to cast on the dramatic situation the light of tragic irony; the heavens are as brass above us, and the beautiful melody refuses to change when the happiness it first sang has turned to sorrow.

And sometimes the composer has written a piece of tragic music and hastily named it after the most powerful tragedy he has read, without troubling to make any real illustration of the subject. As for the story Berlioz told about the origin of this overture in a murderous fit of jealousy, if that was true why did he not call it *Othello*?

No; let us frankly call this overture the Tragedy of the Speaking Basses, of the Plea of the Oboe, and of the Fury of the Orchestra;

and let us be content, in the admirable phrase of Sir Henry
Hadow, to speak of an 'angry sunset' without troubling ourselves
about the cause of the anger.

The overture begins, then, with one of the finest extant
examples of the 'speaking bass' since the recitatives in the Ninth
Symphony.

Ex. 1.

These noble and indignant sentences of the basses are repeated
softly by muted violins. After two pairs of phrases, each pair thus
repeated in its entirety, the strings thrum a naïve triplet accompaniment in pizzicato repeated notes below a melody for the oboe
which I need not quote. It is one of those inspirations, frequent
in Berlioz, which makes you feel that the instrument which plays
it is the most natural thing in the world, and that you have never
heard it before.

This melody is taken up by a soft chorus of wind instruments
with an admirable florid counterpoint for the first violin (Berlioz
has no troubles as a contrapuntist so long as he is inspired by the
tones of an orchestra); and then there is a rich and simple modulation to E flat, where the brass instruments softly sing the whole
melody for its third time, gorgeously accompanied by the whole
orchestra. After this the storm breaks; but, as I pointed out above,
it is not a thunderstorm, whatever else it may be. It consists of
a recapitulation of the Speaking Basses, accompanied by the full
orchestra and punctuated by the impressive drum-figure quoted
above. After the last of the four phrases, two echoing chords bring
the introduction to an abrupt end, and the allegro bursts out with
one of Berlioz's characteristic violently agitated themes, the
straggling phrases of which are, however, held together by an
excellent opening figure (*a*).

Ex. 2.

The course of the movement is simple and quite easy to follow,
though there are several more themes than are quoted here. The
second subject begins with another glorification of the oboe, this
time bringing out a far more impassioned aspect of its pathos.

Ex. 3.

The main points to watch for in the rest of the overture are the first return of the Speaking Basses; the recapitulation, quite formal and regular, of the first and second subjects (Ex. 2 and 3, &c.); the second and greatest return of the Speaking Basses (by way of beginning the coda); and lastly the transformation of Ex. 3 into an outburst of rage for the full orchestra, culminating in that wonderful pizzicato chord which suggests to Strauss that something has snapped in King Lear's brain.

One of the most remarkable things about this unmistakably tragic work is that not only is it written in a major key, but its first four bars are the only important theme that can be construed in the minor mode at all.

CLXIV. 'SCÈNE D'AMOUR' FROM 'ROMÉO ET JULIETTE'

In this work we have a great deal more than the title to assure us that it is intended to illustrate a play of Shakespeare. Yet here too we shall be doomed to disappointment if we look to Shakespeare to explain anything we have failed to understand in the music. Performances of Berlioz's *Roméo et Juliette* as a whole will always be rare; and it is admitted by the greatest enthusiasts that the parts usually heard in the concert-room have little to gain, and something to lose, by their inclusion in the incoherent and unwieldy scheme of the whole: though there are several less-known movements, notably the 'Convoi Funébre', which well deserve a hearing. There is no doubt that Berlioz is inspired by Shakespeare's *Romeo and Juliet*, and by no other discoverable external source; but it is idle to expect that he will be very faithful to Shakespeare when he cannot attend to his own musical and illustrative scheme. He calls the work a Dramatic Symphony, and the term covers a wide range of possibilities; but he makes no attempt to harmonize the conflicting claims of instrumental illustration (both realistic and symbolical), vocal and choral narrative, and dramatic impersonation. As for Shakespeare, Berlioz particularly tells us that the most accurately descriptive piece in the symphony can be successfully played only to a select audience to whom the fifth act of *Romeo and Juliet*, '*avec le dénouement de Garrick*, est extrêmement familier'. You would certainly guess, from its avowed place in Berlioz's work, that the speech of 'l'élégant Mercutio' about Queen Mab filled at least two long scenes, if not a whole act. Throughout the work you never know when or why a chorus, or a solo, is going to intervene with a long explanation, nor whether the voices are going to tell a story, to sing the praises of first love as embodied in 'cette poésie elle même dont Shak-spea-(*vibrato*)-re lui seul, eut le secret suprême'; or whether, as in the introduction to the *Scène d'Amour*, they are going to sing behind the scenes convivial good-nights after the 'bal divin' *chez* Capulet. Meanwhile, or rather at other moments, Berlioz is a consummate magician whose familiar spirits are the instruments of the orchestra; not excluding voices, when he has the inspiration to fill his mind with the sound instead of amateurishly blundering about the sense. And it is a condition of his inspiration that he shall be allowed to be solemnly irresponsible until all the false issues have been boiled away. France is, according to Matthew Arnold, enormously the intellectual superior of England in her possession of 'a public force of correct literary opinion, possessing within certain limits a clear sense of what is right and wrong, sound and unsound, and sharply recalling men of ability and learning from any flagrant misdirection of these their advantages'. It is a mercy that, for all Berlioz's sufferings, no such force availed to check him; for there is hardly a single enterprise of his which does not, as a whole, come under Matthew Arnold's 'class of false tendencies, wasted efforts, impotent conclusions, works which ought never to have been undertaken': and yet if these works had not been undertaken we should have lost several perfect examples of an art purified by Pater's 'hard gem-like flame', which academies have sometimes known to find too hot for them. (Matthew Arnold himself admits as much in the continuation of the passage quoted.)

Such an example is this *Scène d'Amour*. It is obviously inspired by the balcony-scene in the play, and nothing is easier or safer than to identify the cantabile of the 'cellos and other tenor instruments with Romeo, and that of the soprano instruments with Juliet. Other accompanying sounds are equally suggestive of an Italian summer night; and towards the end there is a curious rough interjection of the violins which does not interrupt the sweet flowing phrases of the clarinets, but is undoubtedly intended for the 'noise within' made by the Nurse. This last detail has certainly no artistic value; indeed, it attracts much the same kind of attention as the creaking of a chair; and it is the only attempt at individual description in the whole movement. Berlioz himself rejected the congratulation of the lady who told him that she so easily recognized 'Roméo arrivant dans son cabriolet'. I have often carefully compared the music with the sequence of speeches and ideas in the balcony-scene,

and I am convinced that, after the allegro agitato, Berlioz was not
hampering himself with any notion of making the music follow
their course, except to this extent, that, like the two lovers, it
several times contrives to return and say more after it had seemed
to close. Take it on its own terms, as music, and it is admirably in
character with the balcony-scene. Nobody, for instance, could
possibly mistake it for Tristan and Isolde, nor for Siegmund and
Sieglinde. Like all Berlioz's music (and his style at sixty remained
exactly where it was at twenty-five), it is indisputably young,
civilized, and southern: young enough for Juliet herself, whom
the Italian sunshine had ripened into a woman at fourteen.

The movement begins with a rustling theme in the 'cellos, above
which sighing fragments of melody float for some time. Then,
with some agitation of the rhythm and tempo, an impassioned
theme appears in the horns and 'cellos.

Ex. 1.

The opening theme returns, and leads to Ex. 1 again in a higher
key. This breaks into a high-pitched allegro agitato, all sighs and
palpitations, representing Juliet's agitation at finding herself over-
heard by Romeo. Through this the 'cellos plead in eloquent
recitative, and soon the adagio returns and Juliet speaks to Romeo,
as might perhaps be—

> Thou know'st the mask of night is on my face,
> Else would a maiden blush bepaint my cheek
> For that which thou hast heard me speak to-night.
>
> Dost thou love me? I know thou wilt say 'Ay';
> And I will take thy word; . . .
> I should have been more strange, I must confess,
> But that thou over-heard'st, ere I was ware,
> My true love's passion.

Ex. 2.

It is not possible to be sure that any passage in the music corresponds to this or that speech in the play; but there is no doubt
that Berlioz was particularly fond of the note sounded in the speech
here quoted, which also accounts very satisfactorily for the allegro
agitato just before it. It is just the note which is never sounded by
Wagner's heroines (the Valkyries have in its place the maidenly
pride of goddesses, not of women), and Berlicz has praised
Sacchini to the skies for representing the modest droop of a
Grecian maiden's eyelids by thirds on two clarinets; so that we
can here know his meaning as if we had looked it up in a dictionary.
Nor is there anything crude in its expression; but you must not go
on comparing it with Shakespeare, if you wish to understand and
enjoy it. Shakespeare's poetry is far too definite in ideas and
images to help you to appreciate the success with which this music
calls up its moods without any images at all. I do not mean to
imply that Shakespeare is too 'intellectual' for the situation; but
simply that the way in which his words call up the right moods is
quite incompatible with the way in which the music does so; and
that if you persist in trying to fit the music to the words you will
only end in analysing their prose meaning instead of their moods.
The art of setting words to music so that they can be sung is an
altogether different matter; there the correspondence cannot be too
close: and one of the real reasons why Berlioz produces such queer
hybrids as his *Damnation de Faust*, his *Lélio*, and the whole scheme
of his *Roméo et Juliette*, is that he has no patience with the more
serious problems of the musical setting of words.[1] Let him, then,
have his way; let him set about works which Matthew Arnold
would say 'ought never to have been undertaken', and in sections
of those works he will achieve perfect masterpieces, as unlike each
other as they are unlike anything else in the world.

It is as well to quote one more theme, which, with subtle truth
to Shakespeare, comes to the same conclusion as Ex. 1—

Ex. 3.

&c., as in
Ex. 1.

Good night, good night! parting is such sweet sorrow
That I shall say good-night till it be morrow.

[1] We must be careful! You never know where you are with Berlioz.
Towards the end of March 1935 Dr. Erik Chisholm produced the whole
of both parts of *Les Troyens* in Glasgow, and revealed it as one of the
most gigantic and convincing masterpieces of music-drama.

MENDELSSOHN

CLXV. OVERTURE, 'THE HEBRIDES', OP. 26

If those compositions (including single movements from larger works) which have the qualities of the *Hebrides* Overture were set apart and regarded as the only authentic works of Mendelssohn, there would be no disputing his claim to rank among the great composers. Perhaps when the scholars of a thousand years hence decipher European music of the five hundred years between 1450 and 1950, they will conclude that the pseudo-Mendelssohn of early Victorian idolatry was not the same person as the master of the *Midsummer-Night's Dream*, of the *Hebrides*, and many single movements ranging from the tragic scherzo of the F minor Quartet, to those *Songs Without Words* of which the reckless prettiness achieves real beauty. Even to us Mendelssohn is one of the strangest problems in musical history. Perhaps, in the violent reaction against the worship he received during his life and after his early death, it has been too readily assumed that he had expressed all that was in him. Gluck, Handel, Haydn, Wagner, and Verdi—none of these would have been particularly great names to us if we possessed only the works they had written before they reached the age at which Mendelssohn died. The dangers of a Mendelssohnian facility are notorious; but men of genius, including Mendelssohn, need all the facility they can get. Handel was a fluent composer at the age of eleven, and seemed absorbed in fashionable Italian opera at the age of Mendelssohn's death; while only the immense gulf between Wagner's early and his mature art blinds us to the historic importance of the fact that his worst early work, *Rienzi*, was a world-famous success. *Respice finem* is a very good motto if the end is there for you to look at; but surely no one can say what another thirty years' experience of so eventful a period in musical history would have done for a nature like Mendelssohn's.

The *Hebrides* Overture far transcends the typical praises that Mendelssohn's posterity has consented to assign to him. It is indeed a masterpiece of delicate and polished orchestration, and, as Wagner said, an 'aquarelle' by a great landscape-painter. Also it is perfect in form. But none of these praises imply anything really beyond the comprehension of an age of antimacassars; indeed Wagner's word 'aquarelle' was deliberately chosen by him to deprive his anti-Semitic diatribes of any remains of generosity that might lurk in them.

The perfection of form in the *Hebrides* Overture is the perfection of freedom; it has the vital and inevitable unexpectedness of the classics. It is of loose texture, in a way. Mendelssohn at fifty might have grown into a Handel or a Haydn; he would never have become a Bach, nor even a Mozart. His finish and polish would always have remained his manner, when not his mannerism: it never was his method. Form really meant little to his artistic consciousness: he judged of forms as schoolboys judge of 'good form'; and instead of developing classical forms on vital evolutionary lines as Beethoven developed them, he practised each form only to demolish it by easy short cuts to effect. At the same time it is not true to say that he lacked an infinite capacity for taking pains. Both he and Handel had that almost as markedly as Beethoven. But Beethoven took pains in a reasonable, labour-saving way: his numerous preliminary sketches begin so surprisingly badly because he had the common sense to sketch as quickly as possible, and to waste no pains on a detail until he was sure of its surroundings. Thus, from his first sketch to his fifteenth or so, Beethoven could maintain the freshness of an extemporizer, while at the same time he need never make the same mistake twice; until at last he had only to put into full score what had passed through a scrutiny that had rejected everything which he saw to be unnatural or obscure. With Mendelssohn, as with Handel, all the pains were taken with already finished and polished work; and the result is, no doubt, sometimes worth the trouble it cost. But both composers seem to have achieved their greatest without much revision. More often than not, the result of *six complete versions* is an air like 'Thou art gone up on high', which very few people have ever heard, though you will find it in every vocal score of *The Messiah*. But you will also find a footnote which says 'This air is generally omitted'.

The autograph of the *Hebrides* Overture is in the possession of the family of the late Professor Case, who showed it to me at Oxford in the 'nineties. It certainly contains alterations; but my recollection of it, though vague, is that the alterations are of a kind that happen only in works written at high speed when the material has been prepared rather by the general *savoir vivre* of a receptive brain than by special attention. The beauty of the handwriting extends to the trellis-work which deletes one or two passages which had begun to take the wrong turning or to miscalculate the length of a phrase; and if my memory is correct, one of these passages is the gorgeous modulation to F minor in the middle of the development—but I do not think it amounts to any change of idea. From the moment when Mendelssohn, while actually standing in Fingal's Cave, jotted down, in crotchets and quavers, the first bar—

Ex. 1.

to the moment when he wrote the last pizzicato notes below the mysterious sustained trumpets and the flute with its last fleeting allusion to the second subject (Ex. 3), Mendelssohn was surely occupied chiefly with the unconscious digesting of his impressions of Hebridean scenery, the roar of the waves rolling into the cavern, the cries of sea-birds, and perhaps almost more than anything else, the radiant and telescopic clearness of the air when the mist is completely dissolved or not yet formed.

It must be confessed that Mendelssohn never showed any interest, hardly even an 'intelligent' interest, in folk-music. The scherzo of the Scotch Symphony got as far as a partly pentatonic tune with a distant and probably accidental likeness to 'Charlie is my darling'. What really interested Mendelssohn was scenery. There his mind expanded without that sense of duty which appears in his naïve and genuine expressions of reverence for the contents of the Tribuna in Florence; expressions which prompted Samuel Butler to one of the least good-natured passages in all his writings. Yet even in Italy, Mendelssohn confessed that he could not be bothered to look at Roman ruins when he could contemplate the ruins of a rocky shore. Mendelssohn may have created conventions; but the theory that he himself was conventional will not fit the facts of his life and letters. He was far too industrious and public-spirited to do himself justice as an artist before his career was cut short.

The reason why I have quoted only the first bar of the first theme is the fact (almost without parallel except in such rich streams of melody as the finale of Brahms's First Violin Sonata) that the continuation of the theme is different every time it recurs. It is true that this is mainly a case of building up long passages out of repetitions of a single figure; but the constant difference between fine art and machinery is that the machine repeats its action as long as you keep the power on, whereas in the work of art the long passages owe their noble proportions and their beauty to the single figure. Thus our Ex. 1 makes phrases of different and even contrasted type every time that we think we are listening to its symmetrical recurrences.

Ex. 2 shows an important transition theme, in which I mark with letters certain figures that are used in other combinations.

Ex. 2.

Ex. 3 is the second subject—in its first and complete form quite the greatest melody Mendelssohn ever wrote.

Ex. 3.

In the recapitulation this deep melody is given to the clarinets, and its new serene tone has always attracted attention. Yet few commentators have noted that it completely diverges from Ex. 3 at the sixth bar. Shortly afterwards the lively coda breaks in with material that for several lines owes nothing to any of the themes, and so throws the final peroration of Ex. 1 into admirable relief. Perhaps the most surprising stroke of genius comes at the very end. The trumpets have entered pianissimo during the height of the climax, so that their long note is heard only between the crashes, while the figure of Ex. 1 descends into the darkness, and a quick allusion to Ex. 3, in the minor, flies upwards and away.

CLXVI. OVERTURE, 'CALM SEA AND PROSPEROUS VOYAGE', OP. 27

The inspiring cause of Mendelssohn's *Meeresstille und glückliche Fahrt* is a short poem or pair of contrasted poems by Goethe. Neither in English nor in German does the mere title indicate the meaning of the poems to the prosaic modern reader, who naturally thinks of the calm sea as the essential condition of a good channel crossing. But the poet's sea voyage is not by steamship, and his calm sea is an anxious matter. 'Deep silence broods over the waters; the sea rests without movement; and the mariner is troubled at the sight of the smooth levels around him. No breath of air from any quarter; the deathly silence is awful; throughout the enormous distance not a ripple stirs.' Mendelssohn's treatment of this part of Goethe's poem clearly resembles that of a very little known work of which I have only once heard a performance, and which there is no reason to suppose Mendelssohn himself had seen, though it had been in existence for some years; namely, Beethoven's choral setting of the poems, op. 112. It is interesting to see how the two conceptions begin to diverge when the essential condition of the prosperous voyage comes. Both composers are delightfully realistic on quite different lines when they depict the rise of the wind.

Beethoven, who is composing a setting of the actual words for
chorus (a medium in which he was never fully in practice), is
severely restricted, and the words have not much to gain from
choral expression. 'The clouds are torn apart, the sky is clear, and
Aeolus takes off the chains of anxiety. The winds rustle, the sea-
man bestirs himself; hasten, hasten! the waves divide; the distance
approaches; already I see land.' Beyond the contrast between a
slow and a quick tempo, and the possibility of some *piano* echoes
and repetitions by semi-chorus, there is very little chance of building up the vocal setting of the Prosperous Voyage into more than an
appendix to the Calm Sea. The opportunity is far greater for a
purely instrumental piece; and accordingly, as soon as Mendelssohn
has broken into the profundities of the calm by a faint breath of
zephyr in the flute, all the conditions are ready for a first-rate piece
of broadly impressionistic music. It is unnecessary to quote the
themes, though there are several of them; one very familiar figure
as old as the hills has been explicitly quoted in a passage of the
highest poetic power in the Romance of Elgar's *Enigma* variations.

Speaking generally, it is quite ridiculous to regard Mendelssohn
in this work, and in several others among his ripest conceptions, as
proceeding on orthodox classical lines. There is no doubt that the
work is a classic; but its form is entirely peculiar to itself, and the
clue to it is Goethe's little poem of which I have given the prose
meaning. An amusing and effective point in the whole scheme is
the pompous triumphant finish, not in a quicker tempo but allegro
maestoso twice as slow, indicating not only the sight of land but the
arrival and the welcome (evidently official) given to the voyagers.
But before we allow ourselves to smile a superior smile thereat,
we had better wait for the last three chords, which are a poetic
surprise of a high order.

CLXVII. OVERTURE TO 'RUY BLAS'

The Mendelssohn of *A Midsummer-Night's Dream* is, both in the
overture and in the rest of the music, so wonderfully and classically
attentive to his Shakespeare that I could not help forming high
hopes that the popular and effective overture to *Ruy Blas* would
appear in a new light to a listener who knew 'what it was about'.
Alas! Victor Hugo's play, which I have just read with much edifica-
tion, has not more than enough in common with Mendelssohn to
show that though the composer was undoubtedly writing apropos
of it (the play was produced in 1838, the overture in 1839), his

attention to it was perfunctory. It might have made as good an
opera as *Hernani*, or even as *Le Roi s'amuse* (alias *Rigoletto*); and if
Mendelssohn, after the failure of his juvenile *Hochzeit des Camacho*,
had had the good fortune to be induced to make an opera of *Ruy
Blas*, his attention would have been aroused, assuredly with
masterly results, to many interesting musical resources which, as
fate ruled, escaped him. The wonderful and profound second
movement of his F minor Quartet persuades me that he might even
have mastered the note of tragedy, which Hugo certainly could
sound. But Mendelssohn never, until that latest of his works,
distinguished it from the agonies of a lost purse or missed railway-
train; and Hugo's conspirators could have kept no secrets if they
had been as fussy as the main theme of the *Ruy Blas* overture
(Ex. 2, overleaf). I have nothing against that theme as an effective
musical expression of irritability; but the kind of person it fits is
not to be found in a play where everybody is a conspirator in some
sense, and where the outcome is inevitably tragic. Mendelssohn's
Ruy Blas overture is a piece of vigorous and effective music which
has well earned its popularity with audiences that know nothing
about its subject. And I can assure the listener that audiences may
continue with quiet consciences in that ignorance. Mendelssohn
could not abide Hugo's histrionics: he never realized their close
affinity to his own, and if he could have had his way, the Overture
to *Ruy Blas* would have had no other title than that of the pension
fund for the benefit of which it was written. Any story that this
overture can suggest to a reasonable music-lover will probably fit
the music better than Hugo's play. What do these famous fate-
laden opening chords import, with their dramatic later reappear-
ances in changed harmonies?

Ex. 1.

It is true that the first words of the play are an omen which fore-
tells fatal developments; the villain, Don Salluste, calls to his
lackey:

'Ruy Blas, fermez la porte,—ouvrez cette fenêtre.'

And later on, when the lackey is distinguishing himself as a brilliant
and masterful cabinet minister, and prospering in his love affairs
with the Queen, the villain reappears in secret, and compels Ruy
Blas, by mere force of past habit, to shut a window for him. But on
neither occasion can Don Salluste have given orders to servants in
a tone as loud as the forte of two trumpets, three trombones, four
horns, and all the lower wood-wind. In a play fairly well supplied

with stage directions we are not even told that he raised his voice:
indeed at the beginning he himself continues by remarking that
everybody is still asleep. We cannot ascribe to music the power of
telling the listener (without collateral evidence) that it is representing reverberations in the soul instead of the sounds that caused
them. So, if we must think of anything but music, we may just as
well regard these chords as announcing the massacre of St. Bar-
tholomew, or the anarchism of anabaptists, or any similar assets
of the Scribe-Meyerbeer tradition; and let us be thankful to
Mendelssohn for producing his effects in terms of art so clean and
genuine. What he has in common with Hugo is a Byronic *élan* and
a technical virtuosity that are sometimes distractingly amusing.
Irreverence suggests that Mendelssohn's admirable staccato second
theme (Ex. 3, below) is inspired by Hugo's amazing jugglery with
alexandrines, which he can keep in regular movement while
dividing them syllabically between different persons. When the
Queen sends Don Guritan on a distant errand to prevent him
fighting a duel with Ruy Blas, the climax, stage-direction and all,
is deliciously Mendelssohnian. Here is the last of four similarly
divided lines; you and a friend should practise reading it together
in strict time. (G = Guritan; R = the queen.)

(G) Je . . (R) Non. (G) Mais . . (R) Partez! (G) Si . . (R) Je vous
    embrasserai! (*Elle lui saute au cou et l'embrasse.*)

The rest of Mendelssohn's themes begin as follows; the main
allegro theme—

Ex. 2.

a violent transition theme which I do not quote; the second
subject, true enough to the play in its first timid staccato and in
the low-pitched cantabile that afterwards holds it together—

Ex. 3.

and an energetic theme which is destined to bring the overture to
a brilliant triumph utterly unlike anything in the play—

Ex. 4.

for Ruy Blas, though he triumphs morally, thwarting the vile conspiracy and saving the Queen's honour, conquers only in the moment of death, leaving the Queen to lifelong remorse. Not so does Beethoven illustrate the salvation that Egmont died for; he keeps it outside the tragedy. It would be amusing to write a new programme for Mendelssohn's overture; it would associate the brazen chords with some formidable and recognizable emblem of power, it would deal with persons not essentially tragic, and it would end with every really nice dog in triumphant possession of his bone.

CLXVIII. OVERTURE TO 'A MIDSUMMER-NIGHT'S DREAM'

Just before the war great admiration, stimulated by friendly controversy, was excited by a performance of Shakespeare's *Midsummer-Night's Dream*, in which the setting was neither the realistic illusion theatre of our intellectual nonage, nor the austere endeavour of the Elizabethan Stage Society to get Shakespeare's half-open-air circus under the roof of a modern London playhouse. The setting was entirely modern, and perhaps best classified as 'expressionistic'. There was no nonsense about it, and not even Shakespeare's poetry (to say nothing of his verse) was sacrificed. The fairies, whose representation was the most heterodox feature of this distinguished production, had not only golden clothing but golden faces and hands; and the effect was by no means unfairylike; indeed it was an excellent stimulus to the imagination of an audience that must always be severely strained by the necessity of having to accept as fairies a troupe of actors whose dimensions are reckoned in irreducible feet instead of elastic inches. (Oberon and Titania are, of course, full size; but Master Cobweb is supposed, by Bottom, who knew a thing or two, to be in danger of getting himself soused with honey from the bag of a bee, while the stature of Puck varies from that of a treacherous three-legged stool to something small enough to escape notice in a punch-bowl till his mischief has made the drinker sputter.)

New music was composed for this production, for it was agreed on all hands that in the circumstances Mendelssohn's music would not do. Now for any conceivable production of *A Midsummer-Night's Dream* Mendelssohn's music will 'do' exactly as well as Shakespeare's poetry. Mendelssohn's worst music is out of fashion; but the sifting of good from bad in the voluminous output of a spoilt man of genius is not a task that can be entrusted to snobs; nor can it be simplified by assuming that every turn of phrase which is familiar to us in the bad works is intrinsically bad wherever it occurs. There are three sufficient reasons why, until we possess a musical civilization in Great Britain, Mendelssohn's music will not 'do'; first, because (apart from the rising generation of opera-goers) the British playgoer is trained to treat music and musicians as the dirt beneath his feet; second, because no British non-operatic theatre-orchestra is a third of the size necessary for a decent performance of mature classical orchestration; and last, because, doubtless with exceptions that it would be invidious to name, the British actor-manager is more impenetrably ignorant of music than any reputable musician has ever dared to be ignorant of literature and drama.

As to Mendelssohn's music to *A Midsummer-Night's Dream*, let us take it at its most bedraggled and humiliated moment. Neither the greatest music nor the greatest poetry in the world was ever meant to stand the strain that custom has put upon *The* Wedding March. It has stood the strain remarkably well, and would have suffered no strain at all if performances of it had been restricted by law to the exact full orchestra for which Mendelssohn composed it. It is festive and regal, and, to all appearance, quite unromantic. It precisely suits Duke Theseus and his Hippolyta, who are neither more romantic nor younger than any favourable specimen of an Elizabethan Lord of the Manor with his Lady; and the wit of man has never devised a less banal third term between Fairyland and the efforts of Bottom's troupe. Now, how many people, even among music-lovers, know why the Wedding March, being in C major, begins with a plunge into E minor? The reason is that after Theseus breaks up the Bergomask dance, with the speech beginning, 'The iron tongue of midnight hath told twelve', and continuing, 'Lovers, to bed; 'tis almost fairy time', the march is resumed as the court makes its exit; and the music fades into distance until the E minor opening phrase resolves itself into the fairy theme of the overture when the torchlights are gone and Puck and the fairies appear. Only an experienced opera company can time such things efficiently; and still more hopelessly out of reach of the British stage is the wonderful music scattered through the dialogues in the forest scenes. The trouble is not that our actor-managers do not want music; on the contrary, their custom has often been to demand an almost operatic continuity of musical gutter-scrapings. But until the British Empire has got rid of its tradition that to be musical is to be illiterate, and that the dignity of literature accordingly depends on being unmusical, we shall do well to confine our case against Mendelssohn to works which we are in a position to criticize intelligently.

The composition of the overture to *A Midsummer-Night's Dream* occupied Mendelssohn for a year, during which he attained the age of seventeen. The rest of the incidental music was written four years before his death, and in that music Mendelssohn has recovered the unperturbed instincts of his boyhood.

The first theme—

Ex. 1.

obviously represents the fairies; but the overture does not tell us all about the mysterious opening chords, as we shall find in the play, when Titania awakens to fall in love with her monster.

Another mysterious chord that occasionally interrupts the fairies' dance—

Ex. 2.

is not over-familiar, even in more recent harmonic styles, and (though easily explained by classical theory)[1] was far beyond the scope of any of Mendelssohn's contemporaries. (Beethoven was still writing his last quartets in 1826.)

The world of festive daylight bursts abruptly into the Dream—

Ex. 3.

and soon the horns of Duke Theseus's hunting party resound.

Ex. 4.

Through the ensuing triumphant strains may be heard a strange bellowing tone, bovine rather than brazen. It is the voice of the ophicleide, literally, as well as Shakespearianly, the Bottom of the brass instruments as known in 1826. Composers were already beginning to feel that three trombones could not by themselves produce a harmony that was essentially more than a group of middle parts. The first bass instrument used to supply the want

[1] A reviewer has pointed out its use by Mozart in Così fan tutte.

was the serpent, an S-shaped wooden affair with holes. Presumably this is what Mendelssohn first wrote for here, for he still uses
it in *St. Paul*. But by the time this overture was published (the parts
in 1832, the score in 1835), the serpent had been improved into a
brass instrument with keys, and the pundits of Kneller Hall (after
consultation, no doubt, with the Professors of Greek at the four
Scottish and principal European Universities) had translated the
words 'Keyed Serpent' into 'Ophicleide'. Even in its improved form
the instrument was a ridiculous bass for any sober harmony of trombones, and Berlioz lived long enough to direct that in all later editions
of his works it should be replaced by the bass tuba;[1] a situation
summarized half a century later by the poet Lewis Carroll, who, far
from writing nonsense, obviously referred to Berlioz in saying

'He thought he saw a rattlesnake which questioned him in Greek;
And when he looked again, it was the middle of next week.'

It would accordingly be the height of researcher's folly to hunt
up genuine serpents and ophicleides for performances of *St. Paul*
and *Elijah*. But for *A Midsummer-Night's Dream* the ophicleide is
essential: the tuba can no more replace it than Philostrate, Duke
Theseus himself, or an efficient and conscientious police-sergeant
could replace Bottom. There is no more overwhelming proof of
the boy Mendelssohn's genius than his one perfect use of this
hopeless failure among would-be orchestral instruments.

The ophicleide soon asserts itself in an impudent proleptic
plagiarism from Rachmaninoff's celebrated Prelude in C sharp
minor ('this prophecy shall Merlin make, for I live before his time',
as the Fool said in *King Lear*). The music proceeds in orthodox
sonata form to B major, the dominant, and subsides into a placid
second subject which may safely typify Hermia and Helena.

Ex. 5.

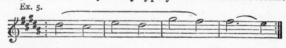

Modern criticism has discovered this to be somewhat school-
girlish; which is precisely true of Hermia and Helena, and is
essential to their charm. The horns of Elfland, not too faintly
blowing, alternate with a suave cadence—

Ex. 6.

[1] Not always: see Mr. Tom Wotton's excellent little book, *Berlioz*
(O.U.P.), for corrections on such points.

which grows in girlish enthusiasm until the climax is overtopped by less elegant strains.

Ex. 7.

Many a talented boy besides Mendelssohn would have enjoyed devising a musical suggestion of Bottom's ass's head; but who else would, seventeen years before writing the rest of the music, have noticed even the existence of his Bergomask Dance and seized the opportunity of incorporating the human aspirations of the whole troupe by combining the two ideas? One of the marks of mature genius is that, within the hypothesis of its art-forms, it is never inattentive. Not all things are relevant to its attention, and it would be useless to urge the authority of Shakespeare in support of any claims Czechoslovakia might urge upon the League of Nations to obtain command of the sea. So we should not find Mendelssohn's accuracy damaged by the discovery that the true Bergomask Dance is not in rhythms of the bourrée type, as Mendelssohn has it, but is really more closely allied to the pavane. This discovery, by the way, is a pure fiction of my own; but plenty of music has been written or compiled for Shakespeare on the lines of such scholarship without the slightest attention to dramatic moods and situations; as if poor Bottom and his colleagues were more likely to know the correct meaning of 'Bergomask' than the correct meaning (than which nothing was farther from their seraphically innocent thoughts) of 'there we may rehearse more obscenely and courageously'.

After the Bergomask Dance the hunting-horns of Theseus make a triumphant end; upon which the fairy themes return suddenly, and a wonderful development takes us deep into the darkening forest, where sudden sounds, at first startling, grow fainter, and more terrifying the fainter they grow; until at last, with the cadence of Ex. 5 in a mournful minor key, poor Hermia, 'never so weary, never so in woe', lies down exhausted to sleep on the ground. (I could have sworn that this passage is used in the incidental music at those words; but the probability of such a use has deceived me, and I find that Mendelssohn has other threads in hand at that point.)

A soft light shines over the last minor chord. It is the first of the four fairy harmonies; and the ensuing recapitulation, very regular

in form, is full of wonderful new sounds. Indeed, throughout the
whole overture there is not a bar of merely conventional, hardly
even of normal, orchestration, though every first principle is
beautifully illustrated. The outburst of Ex. 3 is omitted, as it is
bound to recur, now in the tonic, at the end of the second subject
after the Bergomask Dance. The coda is, of course, devoted to
the return of the fairies, with their blessing upon the House of
Theseus and Hippolyta. But who would have thought that the
brilliant tutti-outburst of Ex. 2 was going to be transformed into
a poetic reminiscence of the Mermaid's Chorus in Weber's *Oberon*,
which had just been produced when Mendelssohn was finishing
this overture? Mendelssohn had no very strong memory for the
origin of his melodic ideas; but plagiarism is objectionable only
when the plagiarist can neither remember nor rediscover the point
of his original: and this final inspiration of the *Midsummer-Night's
Dream* Overture is as far above Weber's Mermaids' Chorus as the
fairies of Shakespeare are above the fairies of Planché.

The overture ends with its four opening chords. The fact that the
final drum-roll is not on the bass-note is one of the most consummate subtleties to be found in any orchestration; and the chords are
otherwise more softly scored than those of the opening.

A few years after Mendelssohn had written this overture, he was
travelling in Italy, and, at a party where all the talent and fashion
were gathered together, was drawn into a lively discussion of a
Shakespearian revival—if 'revival' be the term for something that
nobody concerned had ever heard of before. The play in question
was called *Il Sonno d'una Notte di Mezzastate*, and was 'all about
the doings of witches. In it occurred the stale device of a play
within the play, and this internal play was full of anachronisms and
infantilities': whereupon, writes Mendelssohn, 'all the ladies joined
in and advised me not to read it on any account'.

CLXIX. INCIDENTAL MUSIC TO 'A MIDSUMMER-NIGHT'S DREAM'

The first entr'acte is perhaps the most famous and certainly one
of the most typical of Mendelssohn's scherzos. Written, like
the rest of the *Midsummer-Night's Dream* music, many years after
the marvellous overture, it shows in the work of the experienced
man no loss of the spontaneity of the adolescent genius. It is
always praised as a masterpiece of orchestration. Some day, when
current criticism knows a little more about form, we may come
to recognize that the best works of Mendelssohn are not more
remarkable for their scoring than for the Haydnesque freedom of
their form.

There are several themes in this scherzo. The first is a formula professing, like Domenico Scarlatti's openings, to do little more than assert its key.

Ex. 1.

But it proves capable of development and combination with other themes. The main theme of the second group, on the other hand, is a highly organized phrase full of wit and unexpectedness in the ways in which it coils upon itself.

Ex. 2.

It is given to the whole mass of strings in a multitudinous whisper that is as admirable in its 'night-rule about this haunted grove' as the alarming crescendos that mark later stages of the design. The scherzo ends with an astonishing *tour de force* for the flute. Listeners who wish to appreciate what this involves may be recommended to pronounce two hundred and forty intelligible syllables at the uniform rate of nine to a second without taking breath.

At the last chord, the curtain rises, and Shakespeare introduces Mendelssohn to Puck, who cries 'How now, spirit? Whither wander you?' (Two flutes answer with two bars of Ex. 1.)

> FAIRY: Over hill, over dale,
> Thorough bush, thorough brier,
> Over park, over pale,
> Thorough flood, thorough fire,
> I do wander every where,
> Swifter than the moone's sphere.

Fragments of the scherzo accompany the whole dialogue till the Fairy March, that brings in the ill-tempered Fairy King and Queen.

It has been asked why I produce stage music on the concert platform when I express so strong and so evidently conscientious an objection to concert excerpts from Wagner. I have no indiscriminate objection to such excerpts as are intelligible or made intelligible by their method of presentation. My objection is directed against nonsense, whether on the concert platform or on the stage. On some other occasion I shall enter into the details of this matter. Some things in Wagner are reduced to formless nonsense by extraction from their contexts; some are reduced from the sublime to the vulgarly sensational; and some are injured only by a slightly abrupt or perfunctory end. A few pieces really belong to the concert platform, and one, the Paris Venusberg music, is actually out of scale and style with the opera into which Wagner inserted it; a defect which disappears when it is isolated.

My conscience is completely satisfied by performances of dramatic music on the concert platform if the dramatis personae are adequately represented by singers, or, in cases where there is much spoken dialogue, by a narrator who can compress the facts of the action into something not out of proportion to a performance primarily musical. Whole scenes and acts from Wagner's dramas need only the singers themselves, without interruption or explanation, and might reveal to concert audiences much that escapes an attention fatigued by the enormous scale of the whole drama. Brahms, who was by no means the anti-Wagnerian that his friends wished him to be, used often to go to one act of a Wagner opera each day; and I myself found the second act of *Tristan* an experience of new vividness on an occasion when I arrived in town too late for the first act. Some of the greatest dramatic music in existence is almost impossible to produce except in the concert-room. Goethe's *Egmont* is in Germany itself kept on the stage mainly by Beethoven's music, which the German playgoer is musical enough to wish to hear, though the play itself does not attract him. So even in Germany the need is felt of a device for presenting the music in the concert-room with the aid of a narrator.

The *Midsummer-Night's Dream* music of Mendelssohn is in the predicament that while the play is eminently effective in modern British theatres the music is hopelessly beyond the capacity of anything short of a first-rate opera; Mendelssohn having written for a barbarously Early Victorian country in which the subtle distinction between theatre and opera-house was not clearly marked. It was actually supposed in his day, and the superstition lingers in his country yet, that music in the theatre was as good as music anywhere else. Hence the music for the *Midsummer-Night's Dream* is, like that for *Egmont*, written for a full orchestra, needing the utmost care and accuracy in performance. Except for the absence of singing in the dramatic roles, no dramatic company, however distinguished, could possibly cope with it on terms of less equality than those of opera. A whole concert would be needed to present the music completely in an intelligible framework of spoken dialogue and narration. In such a concert the lover of poetry could enjoy as an honest series of quotations a considerable amount of Shakespeare's poetry, and might even learn something about it from Mendelssohn. No literary conscience can possibly be offended by such a presentation, which does not mutilate because it never pretends either to completeness or to dramatic illusion.

The lover of music will certainly learn some surprising things about Mendelssohn. He will find that that much-abused Early Victorian has nothing in common with the Age of Inattention which was about to begin its enormous task, now almost completed, of releasing the fine arts from all responsibilities. Berlioz has told us that parts of his *Romeo and Juliet* are unintelligible to audiences to whom Shakespeare's play, *avec le dénouement de Garrick*, is not extremely familiar. Such erudition Mendelssohn does not demand of his audience. The words of Shakespeare, as known in current texts, both in English (which Mendelssohn spoke and wrote almost perfectly) and in excellent German trans-lations, are enough for him. But how many of us can read poetry as simply and accurately as Mendelssohn reads it? And of those who can, how many artists with anything like Mendelssohn's 'fatal facility' would have the modesty to keep it in check long enough to notice and act upon the words I underline in the last chorus?

OBERON: And this ditty *after me*
           Sing and dance it trippingly.
TITANIA: First, *rehearse* your song *by rote*,
           To each word a warbling note.

Mendelssohn has grasped two essential points here: first, that both Oberon and Titania have here taught the fairies their ditty before they sing it; secondly, that they are to sing trippingly as well as dance trippingly—that is to say, as Titania explains it, a note to each word, not a coloratura. Her own stanza is set legato, which keeps this rule and yet gives ground for her epithet 'warbling'.

You cannot compare this music with the play in any respect or on any detail without finding Mendelssohn completely in touch with his text.

Into an hour it is possible to pack all the music except the scherzo, the Fairies' March, and the accompaniment of the dialogues in which the quarrel of Oberon and Titania is explained and shown. There is no music to the first act; and the scherzo does not make a good contrast immediately after the overture. A larger selection of poetry would be possible by devoting a whole concert to the work: this selection would then interpose some readings from the first act between the overture and the scherzo; would show how the scherzo is continued in the dialogue between Puck and another fairy; and would include the Fairies' March, the quarrel, and the formation of Oberon's nefarious plot with the magic flower of love-in-idleness. But unless some twenty minutes is available for all this, it is better to summarize it in a short explanation and so obtain the excellent and delicate contrast between the overture and the song, 'You spotted snakes with double tongue', with which the fairies sing Titania to sleep.

At the end of that song you may detect the tragic irony beneath—

> Now all is well.
> One aloof stand sentinel.

The poor little sentinel is no match for Oberon, who steals in and squeezes the juice of love-in-idleness into the sleeping Titania's eyes. She is now doomed to fall in love with whatever 'vile thing' Puck contrives to bring to her first waking glance.

Oberon has also charged Puck to seek out an Athenian, Demetrius, who scorns the love of Helena. Both are wandering in the forest on this midsummer night, he in flight and she in pursuit. Puck is to find them and to contrive that when the Athenian youth sleeps he shall awaken, with the juice of the magic flower in his eyes, when Helena shall be the first living creature he sees. A glorious tangle ensues, for Puck finds the wrong man, Lysander, with his true love Hermia: the father of Hermia intended her to marry Demetrius, who is himself in love with her; and her disobedience is punishable either by death or by consignment to that eminently Athenian institution, a nunnery. She has fled to the woods with her faithful Lysander. In modest separation they lie down to sleep. Puck hastily identifies the discourteous churl whom the poor maiden dares not approach. He squeezes the charm on Lysander's eyes. Enter Helena running in pursuit of Demetrius, who runs faster and leaves her. She sees Lysander, and, seeking his help, awakens him. The charm works; he instantly tears passion to tatters in praise of her. First infuriated at what she takes for mockery she soon flies from him in terror, and he pursues.

Hermia awakens from an ominous dream and finds herself deserted. She wanders away in vain search. And now Mendelssohn, in a movement little known to concert-goers, and less known to theatre-goers, achieves one of his most perfect and subtle character sketches. Perhaps the main tragedy in his artistic development is that he did not understand this achievement himself, and in other works mistook its note for that of tragedy. Elsewhere he has taught us to dread the direction *agitato*, and even made us think that, in accordance with a suggestion of Charles Kingsley's, agitation ought to be assigned especially to aunts. But here, just as the school-girlishness of the second theme of the overture is an exact realization of the special charm of Hermia and Helena, so is the agitation of this intermezzo a perfect realization of the quality and quantity of their troubles. If Mendelssohn had never mistaken such things and such persons for Antigone or supposed that chorales and the thunders of Sinai were their appropriate consolations, all might have been well. And here all is well; besides perfect fitness to the human situation he has realized the midsummer madness in a peculiar orchestration, full of strange echoes and still stranger resonances. Possibly one detail of this was in his mind when in criticizing his sister's orchestration he said, 'Don't you know that you have to take out a licence for writing the low B flat for the oboe, and that it is allowed only in cases of witchery or great grief?'

The intermezzo dies away, and there is a desolate darkness before dawn. The dawn brings a comfort which (though marked *Allegro commodo*) does not at first seem relevant. Puck's comment on it is—

What hempen home-spuns have we swaggering here . . .?

These are the Athenian artisans, assembled in dangerous neighbourhood of Titania's bower, to rehearse the play they hope to be allowed to present to Duke Theseus 'on his wedding-day at night'. Puck soon takes control, changes the head of their star actor into that of an ass and so puts the rest to flight. Bottom the weaver, unconscious of the real enormity of his unshaven appearance, thinks that his companions are trying to frighten him. He sings to keep up his courage, and does not notice that something has gone wrong with his nasal resonances. Something has also gone wrong with the beautiful first four chords of the overture, with which Titania awakens. But her ear is much enamoured of Bottom's note. Oberon's charm has worked. If Bottom is astonished by his exalted surroundings his astonishment is so profound as to leave him no leisure but to adapt himself to them instantly. His manners are worthy of Titania's illusion; he accepts her favours with neither shyness nor arrogance, and converses affably with the fairies appointed to wait upon him, guessing shrewdly at the names of their kinsfolk, to whom he sends polite messages. They hail him with fairy trumpets and drums. (Did you know that two flutes can make a first-rate fairy kettle-drum roll?)

In another part of the wood Oberon learns from Puck of this brilliant success. But Demetrius and Hermia appear, and it becomes evident that Puck has made a strange mistake. Hermia is accusing Demetrius of having made away with Lysander, and his protestations are no more acceptable than his love, to escape from which she had braved her father's wrath and fled to these woods. She leaves Demetrius, and he, exhausted, lies down and sleeps. Oberon charms his sleeping eyes so that when he awakens

he may love her who pines for love of him. Puck's task is now to
lead Helena to the spot. She comes, but she is pursued by Lysander, and, as Puck joyously foresees, Demetrius will now awaken
and find in Lysander a hated rival for Helena's hand. Nor will
Helena be any better pleased to find Demetrius joining in a conspiracy to mock her. And so it turns out. Hermia comes in and
shows herself an excellent match for Helena in a scolding bout.
The two men go off to fight a duel. The ladies do not trust each
other's company. Puck, imitating the voices of Demetrius and
Lysander, misleads the gallants round and about until he has
brought them, exhausted, to lie down and sleep within a few yards
of each other. In the orchestra his laughter gradually becomes the
panting breath and dragging limbs of Helena and Hermia, who
also arrive in utter misery at the same place, and, unconscious of
each other's presence, also fall asleep. Puck puts into Lysander's
eyes an antidote given him by Oberon. All shall be well.

And now concert-goers can find out the meaning of the famous
Nocturne with its beautiful horn solo. It is not fairy music; it is
the comfort of rest to tired mortals blest with natural sleep before
an awakening to happy normal daylight. These mortals are not
Olympian, neither are the impassioned rising phrases that break
out in the violins as a contrast to the serene melody of the horn.
But their answer in the far-off pianissimo wood-wind is as super-
human as the midsummer moon, and the whole scheme is as
Olympian as Mozart or Beethoven. Towards the end the tone
becomes fairy-like, for the scene reopens upon Titania's bower.

Dawn is at hand. Oberon, having taken Titania at a disadvantage, has obtained from her the changeling boy who was the object
of his quarrel. He now undoes the charm. She awakens. The
four mortals sleep on, with the blessing of the fairy king and queen.
The day breaks. Hunting-horns announce the approach of Theseus
and his court. They find the sleeping lovers, whom the huntsmen
awaken with their horns. Theseus overrules the objection of
Lord Egeus to the marriage of his daughter Hermia to Lysander,
and ordains that both pairs of lovers shall be united on his own
imminent wedding-day.

The fifth act is introduced by the gloriously squirearchic
Wedding March, the curtain rising at a carefully chosen moment
after the second trio. Of all the entertainments submitted for
choice by the Master of Ceremonies, Theseus, recognizing sincere
loyalty, chooses that of Bottom's troupe. (If Oberon influenced
Theseus in this matter, which we are not told, he did no more than
pay his debt to Bottom as one gentleman to another.) The play
is a great success, in the quiet manner of success at Court where
kid-gloves are sordines to applause, and the audience is inclined

to make audible contributions to the dialogue. But we may be pretty sure that Bottom got his sixpence a day for the rest of his life. The Funeral March of Pyramus is in the same key as that in the 'Eroica' Symphony, but it is simpler in form, and scored for a smaller band, consisting of a clarinet, a bassoon, and a pair of kettledrums. The Bergomask Dance, which Theseus chooses in preference to an Epilogue, is based on the donkey theme of the overture.

At twelve o'clock Theseus stops the dance, and the royal procession makes its exit to the receding sounds of the Wedding March. These magically become the fairy theme of the Overture as Puck enters upon the now darkened stage. The fairy king and queen enter with all their court. During the first four chords of the overture Oberon and Titania dictate to the fairies what they are to sing. They 'sing and dance it trippingly', pronounce their blessing on the house, and depart. Puck delivers his epilogue through the first (and last) chords of the overture.

SCHUMANN

CLXX. 'CARNAVAL', FOR PIANOFORTE SOLO, OP. 9 (SCÈNES MIGNONNES SUR QUATRE NOTES)

In the spring of 1887 I heard Schumann's *Carnaval* played as it will never be played again. Another musician, whom Edinburgh knows now for many years, will remember the occasion; indeed I can never resist the temptation of any chance for reminding him of it. It was a Saturday Popular Concert in St. James's Hall, London. Madame Schumann was playing the *Carnaval*, and Mr. Hollins was playing Beethoven's B flat Trio, op. 97, with Joachim and Piatti. A misadventure with the tickets led, under good guardianangelship, to a glorious adventure in the artist-room. Joachim was rehearsing Spohr's *Barcarolle* and *Scherzo* with an accompanist. As he walked up and down playing, he pushed with one foot a chair across the room towards a certain small boy who, as he thought, might be tired after the rush up to town.

Thus rested, I heard every note of the concert from a position admirable for sound, dark as any crypt, and hallowed by the passage of the great musicians on their way to the platform. I can remember some details far more vividly than if they were of yesterday—and with the aid of a little self-deception it would be easy enough to spread this vivid quality of memory over my whole after-experience of the music I heard on that day; but truth compels me to say that the details of memory which really date from then are utterly disconnected. The last three bars of the first movement of the Schubert D minor Quartet, and the theme of its slow movement; the five forte notes which recur in *Arlequin*; and the perfection with which Mr. Hollins played the very difficult trills near the beginning of the Beethoven trio; these are the only sounds which I remember with certainty as reaching me in that dark Holy of Holies and not at some other 'Saturday Pop.'. But I believe in the accuracy of my recollections of what Madame Schumann did not do or would not have done; for this was not the only time I heard her. Thus my general memory of her glorious euphony in chord-playing crystallizes into a particularly vivid impression of her rendering of *Chiarina*—which she never played.

The elaborate mystifications of Schumann's *Carnaval* cannot be dispelled in few words, and we must not worry about all the details. I do not now recollect (if I ever knew) why the *Sphinxes*, which give the clue, are placed where they are. They are obviously not intended to be played; though it is recorded of one great player (Herr Hammerfaust von Tastenbrecher, Professor of Pianistics in the University of Weissnichtwo) that he publicly broke five hammers over them. But a rough answer to their riddle, and to the sub-title *Scènes mignonnes sur quatre notes*, is as follows. In the town of Asch lived a lady, Ernestine von Fricken by name. In German musical nomenclature E flat is called Es—which is as much as to say S. Further, by a process easily intelligible to those who have studied medieval music, the Germans, having come to give the name B to the note we call B flat, gave the name H to what we call B natural. (The resemblance of a flat to a small b, and of a natural to a small h is obvious at a glance.) Thus all the letters of the word Asch are names of musical notes. The coincidence that these, and no others, are also the musical letters in the name SCHumAnn could not but strengthen the mystic bond Schumann suspected at the time between himself and the lady of Asch. She appears in the *Carnaval* as *Estrella*. Curiously enough, the piece called *lettres dansantes* (A.S.C.H. S.C.H.A.) is followed, not by *Estrella*, but by *Chiarina*, Clara Wieck, who did not pass out of Schumann's story, but continued to add her own glory to his name many years after I heard her that spring in 1887. The *lettres dansantes* introduce the subject of the second *Sphinx*; which means simply this, that the German name for A flat is *As*, which gives us a new theme of three notes by taking two letters together.

The first *Sphinx* is the musical letters in Schumann's name, which are not used in that order as a theme anywhere in the

Carnaval. Here, then, are the three *Sphinxes* with their interpretation.

Préambule, Eusebius, Réplique, Chopin, most of *Paganini*, and
Pause are the only pieces not based on Nos. 2 and 3 of these
Sphinxes, or on the following modifications which I put into
similar sphinx-like notation.

Schumann, who in after years greatly underrated the *Carnaval*,
and was not always well advised in his sober re-editing of his
early irresponsibilities, confessed that the titles were composed
after the music, and that the music ought to speak for itself.

A *catalogue raisonné*, then, with guiding reference to the *Sphinxes*,
will suffice here.

Préambule, afterwards used extensively and developed in the
Marche des Davidsbündler. *Pierrot* (Sphinx 3), *Arlequin* (Sphinx 3),
Valse Noble (Sphinx 3), *Eusebius*, one of Schumann's three masks
as a journalist. He is of reflective sentimental temper. *Florestan*
(Sphinx 3), the second of Schumann's masks, very impetuous and
incoherent. Meister Raro, the wise old fellow who composes the
differences of Florestan and Eusebius, does not appear in the
Carnaval. *Coquette* (Sphinx 4) is answered by *Réplique*. At this
point the *Sphinxes* are given. One would expect rather to find
them, if not at the beginning, then after *Papillons* which is still
based on Sphinx 3; since after this we come to the new interpretation of the mystic letters. A.S.C.H. S.C.H.A., *lettres dansantes*;
a little waltz on Sphinx 2. *Chiarina* (Sphinx 2) is Clara Wieck,
afterwards Clara Schumann. (She always omitted *Eusebius*, *Florestan*, and *Chiarina* in public performance.) *Chopin*, a wonderful
little portrait of that Chopin who is *not* fairly represented by
violin transcriptions of the Nocturne in E flat. *Estrella* (Sphinx 5)
the lady of Asch. *Reconnaissance* (Sphinx 2). *Pantalon et Colom-
bine* (Sphinx 5). *Valse Allemande* (Sphinx 5) alternates with a
demoniacal performance by *Paganini*, who, turning his violin into
a pianoforte, winds up with a queer conjuring-trick with the pedal,
after which the *Valse* is resumed. *Aveu* (Sphinx 2), pathetically
fluttering with its passion. *Promenade* (Sphinx 5), with many dulcet

whisperings aside. *Pause* is a tumultous passage quoted from the *Préambule* and leading to the *Marche des Davidsbündler contre les Philistins* (Sphinx 2). This League of David was Schumann's not wholly imaginary society of friends pledged to wage war against the Philistines. Their march (a three-legged march in 3/4 time) starts grandly and *Non allegro*, for the business is no joke. A theme from the finale of Beethoven's E flat Concerto—

Ex. 6.

joins the allies; and the pace increases constantly. The poor Philistines are good-naturedly represented by the seventeenth-century *Grossvatertanz*.

Ex. 7.

Twice they waltz stiffly in, through bass and treble, and the pace increases constantly. Twice the ever-pressing throng of reinforcements from the *Préambule* hustles the Philistines away— and the pace increases constantly. At last the League of David is victorious, and the heads of twelve Goliaths fly through the air like twelve turnips, the last one landing (I hope) on a top A flat.

CLXXI. OVERTURE TO BYRON'S 'MANFRED', OP. 115

Like all the most un-Byronic persons of his day Schumann was profoundly impressed by Byron; and *Manfred*, perhaps one of the noblest of Byron's works, inspired Schumann to the noblest of his orchestral music. It really matters very little that Schumann himself was so un-Byronic. The particular Byronic trait that he lacked was nothing but the bluff of a mysterious and mythological wickedness. Schumann had a reverence for sorrow of all kinds, as the root of his keen appreciation of romantic poetry; and romantic poetry attains great heights in *Manfred*. Schumann wrote incidental music to the whole of the play—not quite so much music as was performed in Sir Thomas Beecham's production, and especially not quite so much soft music from the *Kinderscenen* and *Albumblätter*. On the whole it is permissible to say that Schumann's interpretation of *Manfred* in music has a strength and impressiveness nearer to Byron's intentions than the effect of any possible performance of a play in which, as a matter of fact, the

hero almost always appears in a state of complete nervous break-
down. At last he does indeed confront the abbot with:

'Old man, 'tis not so difficult to die.'

Schumann has gone beyond Byron's text in accompanying the
death-scene of Manfred with the sounds of a requiem sung from
the neighbouring monastery, but I see no reason to believe that
there is any substantial contradiction to Byron in thus heightening
the effect of the close. Schumann's reasons are not sentimental.
The monastery is in the neighbourhood of the scene; and it is the
essence of Byronism to admit the existence of what it so ostenta-
tiously defies. The study of the play, with its incidental music,
throws into high relief the power and depth of its overture.

The overture begins hastily with three loud syncopated chords,
which, though standing alone at the beginning, so that the ear cannot grasp the syncopation, would sound entirely different if they
were on the beat, since the players would not so attack them as to
give them their present peculiar breathless expression.

From a slowly moving cloudy sequence of harmonies the following
theme emerges—

and after a while the time quickens slightly, with a sudden forte
in which figure (a) of Ex. 1 reappears. The time continues to
quicken until it becomes an allegro ('In a passionate tempo') and
Ex. 2 is stated with other figures as an impassioned first subject.

The second subject, in F sharp minor and major (=G flat),
contains the following themes—

of which (e) is used in the Requiem at the close of the incidental
music.

Ex. 4.

The second subject, coming to a climax of pride and indignation,
merges into the development, which is founded entirely on its
materials, especially at first (g) and (h). The impressive pause on
a sustained chord for trumpets will not fail to arrest attention.
The dramatic outburst, in the very key of the second subject itself,
of an impassioned transformation of (g) and (f), is the only quotation needed for this section.

Ex. 5.

This leads in broad sequences back to the tonic, preparing for
the return at great length and with fine climax. The recapitulation
of first and second subject is complete and regular, but the second
subject comes to a somewhat greater climax as it merges into
the coda. This consists mainly of an impressive diminuendo on
figure (f) with a new theme on three trumpets.

Ex. 6.   Trumpets. (Wood-wind in 8*ves*.)

The tempo slackens till it reaches the slow pace of the cloudy opening, and the overture ends quietly with fragments of second and first subjects (*e*) and (*c*) in the same mysterious darkness in which it began.

WAGNER

CLXXII. OVERTURE TO 'DER FLIEGENDE HOLLÄNDER'

Der Fliegende Holländer is in many ways the most astonishing of Wagner's earlier operas. We are apt to forget that his *Rienzi* had been an enormous success. *Rienzi* was an opera on Spontini's lines, massive, spectacular, and musically of a coarser fibre than Spontini's. It brought its composer into such prominence that his next work was awaited with widespread curiosity. Would he follow up his great success with a greater, or would he only show signs of repeating himself? The event was utterly without precedent. Wagner followed *Rienzi* with a work that nobody could even pretend to understand. Encouragement came to Wagner from the last quarter that could be expected. Spohr, to whom Beethoven's style was a book sealed with the seven seals of Spohr's own classical prejudices, found matter more to his liking in this new world of which he did not know the manners and customs. He produced both *Der Fliegende Holländer* and *Tannhäuser* with the utmost care at Cassel; and his chief criticism was that Wagner wrote too few rounded periods. In other words, Spohr saw from the reverse side what is the main defect of Wagner's early style. The style has broken away from the classical rate of movement without yet establishing a movement of its own. We take Wagner's mature style as its criterion, and we find that his early style relapses into classical cadences just when it has begun to move on the great Wagernian scale. To Spohr these lapses, when not accompanied by worse lapses of taste, were the main evidences of Wagner's musical talent. The lapses of taste were not worse than those of Meyerbeer, if as bad. In *Tannhäuser* Spohr found a decided improvement in technical matters. This is rather hard for us to discern nowadays; and Wagner's musical taste certainly did not improve between the *Holländer* and even *Lohengrin*. The occasional vulgarities in the *Holländer* happen both to be associated with a vulgar person, Daland, the mercenary-minded father of the romantic Senta, and also to be unpretentious; whereas the worst things in *Tannhäuser* and *Lohengrin* are supposed to be noble and grand. In order to appreciate the extraordinary maturity of the *Holländer*, it is necessary to hear it as Wagner first intended it, as a one-act opera with the music continuing without break during the changes of scene. No butcher's job has ever been more clumsily done than the process by which this opera has been chopped into three acts. Wagner himself is responsible for the butchery, and it is grim evidence of the iron that had entered his soul before his *Wahn* found its *Frieden* in Bayreuth.

The story of the Phantom Ship is worthy of Wagner's unsurpassable powers of pathos and romantic beauty; and his dramatic treatment of it is in advance of his purely musical powers. This is not evident in the overture, a far riper piece of music than the overture to *Tannhäuser*. There is nothing clumsy in the form, which is free and magnificently fluent. To the listener who is not encumbered by a distracting modicum of technical knowledge, Wagner's design will probably display itself straightforwardly. Listeners who wish to call the features of the design by their right names will be glad to know that the vast opening statement, comprising the following two quotations, is an introduction, and that the main body of the overture begins, at the resumption of the original tempo, with Ex. 4. The Phantom Ship appears in Ex. 1, riding through the storm.

Ex. 1.

The Captain of the Phantom Ship has brought upon himself the curse that he cannot die nor rest from his wanderings until he finds a maid who will be true to him. Senta, the daughter of Daland, a Norwegian skipper has brooded over the story of this 'Flying Dutchman', until she can think of nothing else, and cannot feel that her faithful lover Erik has any claim on her. She is always singing the ballad that tells the weird story that enthralls her; and she especially loves to dwell on the phrase that tells of his one hope of salvation.

Ex. 2.

A wailing echo of its last notes—

Ex. 3.

associates itself, in quicker tempi, with the cries of the sailors at their work in stormy weather.

The main body of the overture begins with a theme suggestive of waves.

Ex. 4.

Clearly heard at the outset, it is afterwards seen by the reader of the score more often than it is heard in performance; for the powerful blasts of wind and brass are often too strong for it. The overture now proceeds like a very broad sonata exposition, and introduces a light and lively second group in F with the following Wagnerian sea-shanty.

Ex. 5.

After this, however, the form becomes unorthodox. I believe it to have had a great influence on Schumann in the first movement of his Fourth Symphony. The whole set of themes, from Ex. 1 onwards, with others unquoted, proceeds to develop in broad sequences. These are piled up with magnificent energy, till they reach a climax in the home tonic major, in which we have no recapitulation but a triumphant apotheosis of Ex. 2. In the opera it is only at the last moment, when the Dutchman has already departed in despair, that Senta flings herself over the cliff into the sea and brings him deliverance; but here in the overture we are shown her long-determined resolution, and the force with which she urged herself beyond all mortal scruples. To my mind the most touching thing in all Wagner's earlier works is the sudden calm cadence, when a light shines through the storm and reveals Senta and her phantom lover united on the deck of the Phantom Ship.

CLXXIII. A 'FAUST' OVERTURE

This work is of peculiar interest both for its purely musical qualities and for its historical position in Wagner's many-sided and complex artistic development. It was first composed in Paris in 1840 by the Wagner of *The Flying Dutchman*. In 1855 the Wagner of *The Rheingold* re-wrote it. There is something almost miraculous in the fact that this work achieved its present firm consistency of style, although its creation covered the most unsettled part of Wagner's career. External disturbances were as nothing compared with the conflict not only of style but of aims in the three romantic operas which Wagnerians still insist on treating as if they were the normal antecedents of Wagner's maturity. They were nothing of the kind: they were, on their musical side, the works of a composer who was continually mistaking bad art for good. The history of opera is not primarily, or even largely, the history of good music; and while every word of Wagner's later denunciation of Meyerbeer is not only true but almost temperate from the standpoint of any pure ideal, much of its bitterness arises from the unavowed fact that Wagner himself at the age of thirty-five had still written with most spontaneity and success when he had written most like Meyerbeer. He never imitated Meyerbeer; but in his romantic operas he did undoubtedly enjoy and make the public enjoy just the typical bad things in music that Meyerbeer exploited; and to-day no one with pretensions to musical taste will claim that such things as the end of the overture to *Tannhäuser*, or the brilliant prelude to the third act of *Lohengrin*, can be explained as the innocent lapses of a great artist's early style. They are successful bad music; and their success confused the issue in all the controversies which grew in bitterness as Wagner purified his music and envenomed his prose. By the time he had purified his melody and set it free from symmetrical shackles, the cry was that he had no melody; and there is no denying that the facility of his early melodic invention had been a facility that ran downhill.

It is a wonderful thing that a man no longer young should not only produce the seven most voluminous, highly-organized, and in all respects revolutionary works of art extant, but produce them under the necessity of constantly inhibiting the impulse to write the sort of melody that came naturally to him. Before one can venture to criticize the result, one must learn first to take it as it comes, then to understand how far there is a historic explanation for what fails to explain itself, and lastly to ignore that history where it interferes with our direct view of the result. The problem of Wagner's later melody will then assume something like the shape of Beethoven's later counterpoint, or Browning's diction. No amount of hero-worship will make the Wagner of *The Ring* a facile melodist, Beethoven a facile contrapuntist, or Browning a patient seeker of the fit word in the perfect rhythm; but a reasonably receptive mind will soon be satisfied that at the worst these artists have succeeded in treating these questions as all true art treats the imperfections of an instrument. The imperfections all tend to become useful and expressive qualities. The rough counterpoint strikes fire where smooth counterpoint would glide past unperceived; the melody, shy in repose, violent in movement, and always more at home with instruments than with voices, becomes most human where it is most intractable; and the wrong word in the wrong rhythm marks a stage in the growth of the language when the right man utters it.

There is just enough internal evidence in Wagner's *Faust* Overture to show that it actually was brought into shape during a period when he was being pulled in different directions by incompatible ideals. Only a minute examination and a careful comparison with other works of the period can show this. When we have traced its different origins we shall have accomplished an analysis, which, like all analytical processes, is useless to art or life until we have put things together again. The opening is recognizably by the Wagner of Ortrud and Telramund in the second act of *Lohengrin*; but it is incomparably more powerful, mainly because it is musically terse. Also the weird harmonies of its second figure (Ex. 1 (*c*)) are specifically Wagnerian, whereas Ortrud and Telramund had little beyond fine orchestration to give power to their curses.

Ex. 1.

The beautiful gleam of light that comes in the major mode and seems to suggest the salvation either of Faust or of Gretchen, or at least the hope of salvation, might have had its context anywhere in Wagner's three romantic operas; but here again in this *Faust* Overture it is handled with a terseness and a mastery of form that lifts it far above the sphere of Wagner's early style.

Ex. 2.

Interrupted by a demoniacal yell, it subsides mournfully into an unharmonized and desolate phrase for the violins, in which the main theme (derived from (*a*) in Ex. 1) takes definite shape: there is a crash, and a pause; and then the quick movement begins as follows:

Ex. 3.

This first subject soon rises to a climax, and introduces a vigorous diatonic theme in 'dotted' rhythm—

which may be traced to figure (*c*), but which well bears out the statement that Wagner began to plan this overture after hearing a performance of Beethoven's Ninth Symphony. After this there is a powerful wailing theme given by the oboe in its bitter low register. Through rich modulations this leads to an impassioned close in F, in which key the second subject begins, with a soft melody, exquisitely scored.

Ex. 4.

&c.

Here again terse presentation and masterly continuation disguise from us the historically interesting fact that this melody begins more or less in Elsa's vein. The continuation, with its glorious long-drawn close for the strings alone, can only have been written when Wagner's style was ripe for *The Ring*. Then Ex. 2 reappears in a notation of semibreves and minims suitable to the quick tempo, but really amounting (like the end of the *Tannhäuser* overture) to a return to its original slow tempo. This, by the way, is one of the principal points in which music during and since the 'romantic period' (whatever that may mean) has most radically broken with classical methods. To the classical composer this kind of obliteration of the sense of tempo seemed vulgar; and in the *Tannhäuser* overture we may as well admit that it *is* vulgar, all the more because it is evidently meant to be extremely grand. Why is it not vulgar here in the *Faust* Overture? Just because the quiet string passage, which I believe to be the latest feature in the overture, has already relaxed the tempo; so that the relaxation is not associated with the crescendo at all. This development of Ex. 2 works up to a climax of solemn tragic power, where its slow steps acquire a majesty of their own, which borrows nothing either from the quick or from the original slow movement. When the note of salvation (if that is the right word for it) has become a thundering note of judgement, and its echoes have died away under another demoniacal yell, once more, as in the introduction, it is softly reasserted. One cannot but think of the last line but one of the first part of *Faust*:

Mephistopheles. Sie ist gerichtet!
Voice from above. Ist gerettet!

Then after a few broken chords the first theme (*a*) is developed with admirable terseness in a passage strongly suggestive of the Witches' Sabbath; and this leads back to the tonic in a powerful crescendo, returning to a clearly-marked recapitulation with a climax that can easily be traced to its mighty original, the return in Beethoven's Ninth Symphony.

The second subject (Ex. 4) sails in, a quiet angelic figure floating above a storm-wrack that now and again eclipses it. At last it vanishes; and the wailing transition theme (unquoted), that had originally appeared in the lower octave of the oboe, now enters, for the second and last time, in the full wind-band. The hopeful theme of Ex. 2 becomes a final cry of despair. At last nothing is left but the violins, with a lingering sigh from the first subject (*a*). On the prolonged last note of that figure (C sharp) a shining chord from an immensely distant key poises itself. This wonderful harmony moves calmly towards the tonic major; the violins wing their flight upwards with the rapid figure (*d*) from Ex. 2; and the great work ends in the light of dawn.

According to Wagner's own account, and according to the quotation which he puts at the head of his score, this magnificent movement with all its contrasts was intended to describe the soul of Faust at the culmination of his weariness of life. Gretchen was to be treated, as in Liszt's *Faust* Symphony, in some other and independent movement. But it is impossible to believe that Wagner really confined himself to this programme. The wish to deal with Gretchen separately may have been either cause or result of the conviction that the Elsa-like theme of Ex. 4[1] was not naïve enough for her; but it is very difficult to suppose that that theme has not more to do with *das ewig Weibliche* than it has to do with Faust's own soul. Of course, it is always possible to say that this and the unmistakable representation of the Witches' Sabbath are seen through the medium of Faust's soul. But still, the quotation which Wagner uses as his headline will never cover much more than the opening theme of the whole. Let the reader judge for himself.

Der Gott, der mir im Busen wohnt	The God that dwells within my breast
Kann tief mein Innerstes erregen;	
Der über allen meinen Kräften thront,	Can stir the inmost of my being, Holds all my power at his behest,

---

[1] Dannreuther refers it 'presumably' to some famous lines in which Faust describes the impulse to get into touch with Nature by walking in the woods and meadows. I think it is more respectful to Wagner to doubt his own merely verbal account of this far from simple music, than to suppose that even in his earliest efforts a deliberate intention to get into touch with Nature could result in anything so wide of that purpose.

Er kann nach aussen nichts be- wegen;	Yet nought without marks His decreeing;
Und so ist mir das Dasein eine Last,	And so my whole existence is awry,
Der Tod erwünscht, das Leben mir verhasst.	Life hateful, and my one desire to die.

This essay will have missed its mark if it leaves the reader with the impression that it discovers in Wagner's *Faust* Overture an odd mixture of styles. On the contrary, it aims at showing how an artist of Homeric genius can make a single style, peculiar to a single and perfect work, out of materials and habits which a little investigation shows to be such as a weaker artist could not reconcile with each other at all. Many a Homeric question, many a problem of Higher Criticism, has led to loud assertions about divided author- ship, or loud denials of the very existence of the reputed author, on far less evidence than will in a few centuries suffice to prove that Wagner's *Faust* Overture was compiled by a committee of university dons from fragments of the lost works of Beethoven, Marschner, Weber, Meyerbeer, and Spontini.

CLXXIV. PRELUDE TO ACT III OF 'TANNHÄUSER' (TANN- HÄUSER'S PILGRIMAGE), IN THE ORIGINAL VERSION

By far the maturest part of *Tannhäuser*, indeed the only part of which the music reveals a true Wagnerian power, is the prelude to the third act and the narrative of Tannhäuser's pilgrimage. The prelude, as produced in a performance of the opera, is deeply impressive and fully adequate to its purpose; nor is there any reason why we should dispute Wagner's stage-craft in his reduc- tion of it to its final form in the opera. But a concert piece is a different matter, and we may be allowed to rejoice in the fact that its original form has been preserved. For the final version is the merest summary of the great symphonic adagio which Wagner originally wrote; and in the concert-room such a summary barely escapes producing a patchy effect. In one particular only does the original version seem less clear than the later; and that is in its treatment of the well-known peals of descending scales, which in the final version are much more prominent and seem more clearly to represent the surging up of forces, demonic or natural, and neither good nor evil except as they are mastered and directed. In all other points the original version (published by Novello & Co. in the present century) is far more complete both as a purely musical design and as a piece of musical illustration.

It begins (as in the final version) with one of the songs of the Pilgrims—

Ex. 1.

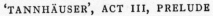

alternating with a theme belonging to the saintly Elizabeth, whose pure love for Tannhäuser redeems him when she dies.

Ex. 2.

The groans of the penitent Tannhäuser are heard in the following figures—

Ex. 3.

   &c.

and the burden of sin which he shares with his fellow-pilgrims is alluded to by these well-known harmonies, which are the first manifestation of the real Wagner in the overture—

Ex. 4.

The saving power of Divine Grace is proclaimed in this severe scale theme—

Ex. 5.

and at this point the original version begins to differ from the final epitome to which Wagner reduced it. A phrase, belonging to the saintly Elizabeth, appears softly in high wind instruments. I will quote it later when it takes more definite shape. The pilgrims' chorus continues for one more phrase, as in the final version. Then, in the final version, the uprush of demonic powers was typified by four bars on the famous figure—

which is so prominent in the overture. Here, in the original version, there is a much more voluminous uprush with no theme at all. It takes nine bars to grow and die away, and then there is a long development of St. Elizabeth's theme.

Ex. 6.

Its extreme simplicity is not quite that of the immense style of
Parsifal, but it contributes to a total impression of this prelude
which is decidedly nearer to that of Wagner's last work than even
the final version of this part of *Tannhäuser*.

Another uprush of demonic forces brings us to a solemn entry
of Ex. 6 in the full majesty of the brass. Here, after 36 bars, we
rejoin the final version. But, after the second outburst of the brass,
the final version continues with eight bars of demonic uprush on
the famous demisemiquaver figure, and then concludes with a
solitary allusion to Elizabeth in heaven and her prayer before the
throne—in fact, with the last twenty-three bars as they stand in
the original version. But this original version has another thirty-
five bars instead of those eight demisemiquaver bars; and the
design is unquestionably broader and clearer both as music and as
illustration. Its merits as illustration constitute, in fact, the very
reason for Wagner's abridgement: the penitent Tannhäuser's
confession, including the awful avowal of his sojourn in the
Venusberg—

Ex. 7.

and the Pope's horrified anathema, are so clearly represented that
they prepare the ground for Tannhäuser's *viva-voce* narrative only
too effectively, and Wagner realized that he could not afford so to
delay and forestall his action. But there is no doubt of the right-
ness of his original scheme as a piece of music; and the pathos of
the saint's dying prayers at the end is here, and here only, given its
full intended effect.

CLXXV. INTRODUCTION TO 'TRISTAN AND ISOLDE'

Of all excerpts from Wagner's later operas this suffers least from
adaptation to the concert-room; except indeed when it is welded
together with the arrangement of Isolde's Liebestod, which is in a
totally different group of keys and only destroys the impression of
the Vorspiel, which, in its turn, is not the most effective preparation

for the Liebestod, or, indeed, for anything but what it was meant for—the whole opera, beginning at the beginning.

But Wagner has furnished three most convincing pages of exquisite scoring and subtle rhythm to round off this Vorspiel in its own proper key; which makes it all the more surprising and regrettable that it is so seldom heard alone with this finish. The *Tristan* Vorspiel, viewed in its own chromatic and subtle light, is almost as continuous and single a process of unfolding the resources of harmony as is one of Bach's simplest arpeggio preludes. The tonic around which all the incessant modulation centres is A, at first minor, and then, in the middle and at the close (as added for concert performance), major. The scheme is simply the growing tension towards, and relaxation from, a climax of passion; and the passion is the love of Tristan and Isolde. All the themes are, in the opera, associated directly with that love, or with the fatal magic potion which caused it—except one figure heard in the bass and here marked (*e*), Ex. 4, which belongs to that dramatic motive of honour betrayed, whereby Tristan and Isolde were impelled by their tragic past to drink what they thought to be Death, but which proved to be the far more terrible Love that was to betray them again.

The principal figures, which arise one by one till they gradually combine and pervade the whole orchestra, are as follows. Most of them, it will be seen, are very closely allied.

Ex. 1.

(b)

(a)

Ex. 2.

(c)   &c.

Ex. 3.

(d)

Ex. 4.

(e)   (e)

&c.

Ex. 5.

(f)

Ex. 6.

The climax brings in the trumpets with (*b*) of Ex. 1. The sudden dying down of the music led originally to another key (C minor), on which the curtain rose to the song of a sailor in the shrouds of the ship that takes Isolde to Cornwall as a captive bride for the king. In the concert version this key is evaded, and the Vorspiel is most beautifully rounded off by a change to slow common time with the theme of Isolde's Liebestod in A major.

Ex. 7.

&c.

Among the many subtle beauties of this most successful of all Wagner's concessions to concert orchestras, the new tonic position given to figure (*b*) at the end is especially happy; it is, of course, transposed from the end of the Liebestod.

Ex. 8.

CLXXVI. PRELUDE TO 'THE MASTER-SINGERS'

The prelude to *The Master-Singers* loses less than most excerpts from Wagner by performance in the concert-room. Its climax is not so perfectly balanced when it can lead only to a final chord as when it leads to the rise of the curtain and the lifting of our attention to a wider world of art; but it is a very complete and highly organized masterpiece of form and texture. Its famous combination of themes I quote—

Ex. 1.   The Song.

The Master-Singers.

for the double purpose of saving space by putting three **examples** in one, and pointing out that its merit as counterpoint **lies not in** the combination of themes (which, unlike classical counterpoint, really do not of themselves combine into complete or euphonious harmony), but in the modest accessory parts (here printed in small notes) which so beautifully smooth away what would otherwise be grievous to Beckmesser.

The prelude opens with the Master-Singers' theme (contained in the bass of Ex. 1) pompously delivered by the full orchestra.

A gentle reflective note is struck by Ex. 2, the figures of which are associated with Walter's love-songs.

Ex. 2.

The dignity of the Master-Singers is resumed in a march, the theme of which will be found at doubled speed in the middle stave of Ex. 1. It leads to another broad cantabile of which an irreverent diminution occurs later on in the treble of Ex. 3. In that form I quote it to save space.

Ex. 3.

Surely she'll re-fuse him! Surely she'll re-fuse him!

In the maiden's place I would not choose him!

The whole exordium comes to a grand close, and is followed by
the substance of an eager conversation between Walter and Eva—

Ex. 4.

which leads, in lovely modulations, to E major. In this key the
Abgesang (or envoy) of Walter's prize-song (seen in the top stave
of Ex. 1) alternates with other love-themes from the song that the
Masters rejected, such as—

Ex. 5.

Excited modulations carry us to the opposite end of the tonal
range, E flat, in which key the Master-Singers' theme is irreverently
diminished by the apprentices, whose rude comments on Master
Beckmesser occupy the bass of Ex. 3. A climax is reached; C major
returns in all its glory, and with it the simultaneous combination
of more than half the themes in the opera, beginning as in Ex. 1,
and developing until, as if by sheer weight, the counterpoint
coalesces into the simple processional version of the middle stave
quoted, and so leads in triumph to the rise of the curtain.

CLXXVII. 'SIEGFRIED IDYLL'

This *Idyll* was written as a serenade for Frau Wagner after the birth
of Siegfried Wagner. (It is said that Frau Wagner very nearly
spoilt the surprise intended for her by becoming anxious about
young Hans Richter, Wagner's amanuensis, who lived in the house,
and who, she thought, was up to no good when he disappeared
every evening—to rehearse this piece.)

The connexion between the *Siegfried Idyll* and the great duet at
the close of the opera *Siegfried* is perhaps more likely to mislead
than to help to an understanding of this unique and purely instrumental work. In scope, in purpose, and above all in movement,
the two things are so entirely different that the allusions made by
the *Idyll* to the opera will not carry us much farther than Virgil's
Fourth Eclogue will carry us in New Testament criticism. Wagner
named his son Siegfried after the hero of his national tetralogy.
The melodies in which Brünnhilde the Valkyrie gave up the
memory of her immortality for the love of Siegfried who had
passed through the fire to awaken her—these themes are woven
with an old German cradle-song into a serenade for the mother of

an infant Siegfried; and what message they have for the public at large is not to be found in the words Brünnhilde sang.

The supreme things in life, the stuff of which tragedies and comedies are made, the *Hort der Welt* which is born wherever old cradle-songs are sung—all these things are within the grasp of great music and great art; but you must leave it to the music, or whatever art it is, to tell you about them; and then you must take the art on its own terms, without attempting to exalt them or debase them by comparison with any other terms. Try to explain the music by other things, and you will achieve nothing but an impertinent intrusion on private affairs, the whole poetic value of which consists in what is sacred because it is universal. Listen to the music as music, and you may have some chance of feeling as Wagner felt when he wrote it.

If one has luck in making one's first acquaintance with Wagner's later style after a familiar acquaintance with the classical types of movement in music, one's first impression will be, quite correctly, that the music is enormously slower and larger in every step it takes. Much of the opposition Wagner met with arose from the difficulty contemporaries had in seeing that his music moved at all. His earlier and most popular works were, in fact, poor and commonplace in composition where they were on old lines, and often vague and lame where they were revolutionary; and the presumption was that his later works, being altogether revolutionary, had no composition in them at all. Nowadays we all know better; and it is almost an arithmetical axiom to us that Wagnerian music moves no faster than the development of a drama, whereas earlier classics, whether instrumental or operatic, had an irresistible tendency to make completely finished and often highly dramatic designs within a space of ten minutes or, at the utmost, a quarter of an hour.

This being so, it may surprise us to find that Wagner's purely instrumental *Idyll* moves almost incomparably slower than the passages in the opera from which its main themes are taken. Eight times as slow is a very moderate estimate. If you know the *Idyll* before you know *Siegfried*, the passages in *Siegfried* will seem to you mere shreds and patches in comparison. The explanation lies in two directions. In the first place, the opera is so enormously larger than the *Idyll* that even a good-sized detached portion will be much more likely to fail to show any definite symmetry or drift; just as a square foot of a fresco may fail to show as much as a square inch of an easel picture. In the second place, in mastering the huge scale of composition he needs for his music-dramas, Wagner has acquired a permanent habit of thinking in that scale and is successful in applying it to 'absolute' music. In short, the

Siegfried Idyll succeeds where practically every 'Symphonic Poem', from those of Liszt onwards, fails. It is a piece of purely instrumental music, quite twice the size of any possible well-constructed move-ment of a classical symphony, and yet forming a perfectly coherent and self-explaining musical scheme. Its length, its manner of slowly building up broad melodies out of constantly repeated single phrases, and the extreme deliberation with which it displays them stage by stage in combination, are features of style that have nothing to do with diffuseness; they are as purely legitimate and natural terms of movement as the terms on which the earth goes round the sun—many times swifter than a cannon ball, yet it takes several minutes to pass its own length. Whatever difficulty has been felt with the *Siegfried Idyll* would be felt with a classical symphony if our scale of time were but slightly altered; and indeed all Beethoven's broadest passages were bitterly resented by those of his contemporaries who thought him worthy to be judged by Mozart's standards.

The *Siegfried Idyll*, then, is a gigantic though intensely quiet piece of purely instrumental music, connected with the opera only by a private undercurrent of poetic allusion. It begins with an introductory building-up of its first theme out of a single phrase. The theme itself is Brünnhilde's yielding to Siegfried: '*Ewig ward ich, ewig bin ich*'; but it does not move at all on the lines Brünnhilde laid for it. It goes its own way in ample leisure and peace, in com-bination with a figure (*b*) associated with Brünnhilde's sleep in her slumber, magic, fire-guarded chamber.

Ex. 1.

It gradually moves like a very indolent sonata movement towards a foreign key (the dominant), where a group of several new themes (not in the opera) constitute quite a rich 'second subject'—

Ex. 2.

ending deliberately with an old popular cradle-song—

Ex. 3.

which the listener cannot fail to identify when he hears it in its bare
simplicity on the oboe, with a tiny accompaniment in slow staccato
descending scales. This accompaniment is undoubtedly suggested
by the myth of the Little Sandman who strews sand into children's
eyes at bedtime to make them sleep.

Then the first theme returns, but is interrupted by mysterious
mutterings from the horns. The violins put on sordines and lisp the
close of the cradle-song; clouds come and go from a land of dreams,
a new and strange light appears, and in a distant key and changed
and quickened rhythm the wind instruments give the theme of
'Siegfried, Hope of the World'.

Ex. 4.

In a passage distinguished, even for Wagner, by its rainbow-
coloured orchestration, this theme is built up in countless short
steps which our memory sees in a long perspective. After some
time the first theme appears above it, as indicated in another position by the lower stave of Ex. 4, and at last a climax is reached; the
violins dash down in a torrent, and then, suddenly, a solitary horn is
heard over a long holding note, with an energetic new theme quietly
played, while a clarinet and a flute break in now and then with the
cries of birds—

Ex. 5.

A rustling theme in triplets is added—

Ex. 6.

These new themes belong to the triumphant finale of the duet in
Siegfried, but the opera text will not help us—nor do they give us
any musical difficulty that needs such help. With them the other
themes very soon combine, the first theme, and Brünnhilde's slumber, and 'Siegfried, Hope of the World,' until a trumpet is heard

rising in triumph to the songs of the *Waldvöglein*. This is not
the nondescript birds that interrupted the new horn-theme, but
the bird whose language Siegfried understood—the bird that
guided him to the Valkyries' rock. The trumpet is silent, and the
music subsides in a glowingly poetic recapitulation (with various
enrichments of detail) of the material which we designated as
'second subject'. The horns croon the old cradle-song until the
Hope of the World is safe in sleep.

SMETANA

CLXXVIII. OVERTURE TO 'THE BARTERED BRIDE'

This brilliant overture is the prelude to a charming opera which is
prominent among the artistic assets of Czechoslovakia. The opera
is on lines of lyric comedy, and no great new light is shed on the
overture by discussing the play. The object of the overture is to
create the liveliest possible comic atmosphere—such as no overture
since *Figaro* has attempted; and also to sound a bucolic note
conspicuously absent from *Figaro*. The liveliness starts headlong
with the running theme which, arising out of the syncopated
opening—

Ex. 1.

runs round like a squirrel in a cage, trying to behave like a fugue
but never getting off its tonic.

Ex. 2.

The bucolic element is supplied by this tune—

Ex. 3.

After it has been worked up as a rumbustious second subject, the
development begins with a quiet reflective passage for wood-wind,
on a slow theme which I cannot trace elsewhere. This throws the
bustle and jollification of the rest into higher relief. Towards the
end also, Ex. 3 goes through quiet romantic modulations. But
the underlying tempo never changes, and the total effect is of
extreme brilliance and speed.

JOACHIM

CLXXIX. OVERTURE TO A COMEDY BY GOZZI

(Notes written for the London concerts of the Meiningen Orchestra,
November 20, 1902)

Even to those who best know and admire Joachim's compositions
this overture will come as a surprise. It was published in 1902 by
Simrock, but was composed (according to a note at the foot of the
first page) in the autumn of 1854, after reading *two* plays, *König
Hirsch* and *Die Frau eine Schlange*. This would seem to indicate
that the title *Zu einem Gozzi'schen Lustspiel* is generic rather than
particular; so we need not trouble ourselves about questions of
'programme music'. Joachim was from the first a master of pure
musical form, and far more of a pioneer in orchestration than many
composers whose tendencies were revolutionary.

Where this overture surprises those who know Joachim's other
works best, is in its lightness of touch and play of fantastic humour.
Yet the noble melancholy of Joachim's other compositions is akin
to the humour of this musical fairy tale. As well take a liberty
with Titania or Ariel, as mention this overture in the same breath
with anything trivial or foolish.

The orchestration has immeasurable wealth of finished and
essential detail. Joachim had acquired early in life an intimate practical experience in handling the orchestra, which enabled him to give
aid in the scoring of Brahms's First Pianoforte Concerto. And the
classic wealth of themes is of a piece with the orchestration. Hence
I give many quotations; but they will not be enough. Let us
think of Joseph Haydn—the real Haydn—not the powdered wig
filled with jejune square-cut tunes arranged in sonata form. That
person has no existence outside text-books. The real Joseph is a
very great composer who left the world early in the nineteenth
century for a generation or so, but then returned with a different
surname, playing the violin as it had never been played before,
and not entirely giving up composition. For instance, he wrote an
overture in his most Haydnesque manner, availing himself of all
that has happened in music since 1808, and beginning as follows:

Ex. 1.

Two allied subsidiaries in D minor and its dominant—

lead to a fortissimo counterstatement of all three themes. Note the double meaning of (*b*) in the new accompaniment of No. 1, whereby it takes the place of (*a*)—

and note also the snarl of hand-stopped horns. The order of keys is so arranged as to lead to the relative major, where we have a second subject that begins gently (*un pochettino meno mosso*) as follows—

This gives rise to a tributary—

which is varied in triplets and demisemiquavers with a whimsical effect, leading to a new theme in the minor and closely allied to the first subject.

Suddenly this bursts out in a blustering tutti; and figure (*d*) is turned into a long passage beginning *piano* and working up in triplet and demisemiquaver variations till it again pervades the orchestra with bustling noise. An important cadence-figure with horns in dialogue with the strings—

Ex. 7.
(*f*)

brings the exposition to a close, with a romantic and sudden decrescendo. The last chords have trills which become the following rhythmic figure, reminiscent of (*b*)—

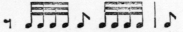

which takes the shape of (*a*) and leads back to No. 1 in its original key. After twelve bars this new rhythmic variation of (*a*)—

angrily interrupts, and carries us to A flat, where No. 2 is developed and passes in large sequences to A flat minor and C major. Here (*e*) is combined with Ex. 7, which is expanded into a four-bar phrase by new matter.

Ex. 8.
(*e'*)

That continuation must surely have influenced Brahms in the rondo of his A major serenade which was written a few years later.

Ex. 8*a*.

Ex. 8 moves broadly from key to key, with unfailing variety of tone-colour; e.g. the surprising behaviour of the trumpets and

horns on two occasions. Then a new countersubject (*x*) to figure
(*e*) attracts notice, after the second outburst of trumpets.

This new figure (*x*) is soon heard climbing quietly into the
heights, where it becomes a filmy cloud, while No. 7 (*f*) alone
appears pianissimo below and is treated by inversion.

Again figure (*x*) rises up like an evening mist; and the inversion
of (*f*) becomes augmented as well, while the semiquavers of
(*x*) slacken to triplet quavers.

(*f*) augmented and inverted.

Nothing is more characteristic of Joachim, nor more decisive in
its influence on Brahms, than such dreamy processes of quiet
expansion.

Another step brings us to the dominant of B flat. But this is the
key, not of the first, but of the second subject. Yet the first subject
steals back in the tonic, out of the cloudy residue of (*x*), in the
most subtle and imaginative passage in the overture.

Note the Trumpets, Horns & Drums.

Watch the rising Bass.

The recapitulation is quite regular, the second subject being brought into the tonic by rearranging the keys of the first subject and omitting its counterstatement.

I need not quote the short coda which consists of the running away (*allegro molto*) of the first theme, and the grotesque treatment of its last figure (*d*). Any listener who finds that the end comes just where he expected must be a person of infinite acumen. It may be permitted to hint that the end is not solemn, and has no pronounced tinge of melancholy. Those of us who can remember how the Joachim Quartet used to play Haydn's one-foot-in-the-air abrupt endings will find no difficulty in the theory of reincarnation when they listen to this overture.

DVOŘÁK

CLXXX. SLAVONIC RHAPSODY IN D MAJOR, OP. 45, NO. 1

Dvořák's three Slavonic Rhapsodies show his naïve genius in its most amiable light, when his mastery and inventiveness had already attained ripeness and the world had not yet told him how naïve he was.

Muffled drums begin with a rhythm that slowly puts itself together, and then the wood-wind begin a rustic melody in Dvořák's characteristic trailing cast of sentence.

Ex. 1.

The tone is reedy to astringency, like an idealized harmonium; and Journalism itself knows not what would have been said by the anti-Brahms critics if Brahms had ever scored so thickly and roughly. The 'Brahminen' would probably have made matters hopeless by denying the thickness and roughness of this passage; whereas the real defence is that it is typically rustic.

After a spacious exposition with picturesque companion-themes in foreign keys, and grandioso climaxes in which Dvořák is at least as majestic as a Mace-Bearer, there is a change to a darker key, and a march sets in.

Ex. 2.

Its manner is dignified as far as the quotation goes; but Mace-Bearers should not be required to hustle; and the procession, which we may take to be mounted, has an alarming tendency to stampede.

Through all the vicissitudes of humour the music remains inveterately poetic, and every modulation, every device of form, is perfectly balanced. The obvious goal of the design is to combine the two themes in brazen triumph.

Ex. 3.

Yet the end is an exquisite die-away in the clouds, over the pulsations of the rhythm of the muffled drums.

CLXXXI. SLAVONIC RHAPSODY IN A FLAT, OP. 45, NO. 3

One of the delightful things about Dvořák is that he never knows what he ought not to like. Meyerbeer's Prophet sings the praises of the Eternal *comme David ton serviteur*, through the mouth of Caruso, and to the accompaniment of two harps and three kettle-drums. Only persons deeply conscious of having recently acquired Good Taste can remain unthrilled by this. Dvořák probably heard it and was duly thrilled before he wrote his A flat Rhapsody. But perhaps 'its native ingenuity sufficed' his 'self-taught diaphragm'.

Ex. 1.

Dvořák loved the smell of incense. Whether he loved it best on the stage or in church we cannot tell. It is less often found on the stage, and seldom so well managed there as in church. In this Rhapsody it is as harmless as the smell of peppermint.

Ex. 1 is followed by symptoms of distress which, like the frown on Dolly's brow at the beginning of *You Never Can Tell*, might conceivably indicate 'a sheep in wolf's clothing'. But that frown was merely the last trace of the agony of tooth-extraction. It cleared off, 'leaving her brow as innocent of conviction of sin as a kitten's'.

Dvořák's unregenerate theme is no such well-informed person as Dolly, but it is quite as lively.

Ex. 2.

Another theme thinks itself as grand as does the King of the Jolli-ginki in his Royal European Top Hat.

Ex. 3.

The vicissitudes of these themes are picturesque and emotional. Samuel Butler said, in one of his less amiable moods, that 'nobody was ever so good as Darwin looked'. The return of the tempo of Ex. 1 is so solemn with its gorgeous deep tones and throbbing drums that we are almost afraid that Dvořák is about to degenerate into an Earnest Person. Such blasphemy, however, never entered his innocent mind. Cheerfulness breaks in again with a new theme, though the design ought long ago to have been closed to anything but Logical Developments.

However, the door is vigorously belaboured until it opens to .he stranger, who lounges in with an *air conquerant*:—

Ex. 4.

After this not all the Parsifal-bells in Dvořák's *vie de Bohême*—

even in combination with Ex. 1 in full peppermint-strength, will make us anxious. A faint echo of the end of the slow movement of Beethoven's C minor Symphony brings a Shakespearian breath of fresh air to the close.

RIMSKY-KORSAKOV

CLXXXII. CONTE FÉERIQUE, OP. 29

I have not been able to identify the fairy-tale told by Pushkin which is the subject of this very rich specimen of Rimsky-Korsakov's exquisitely clear and brilliant tone-painting. With all its characteristic simplicity in phrasing and composition, it has a genuine freedom of form and a variety of matter which suggests that it is not confined to any one fairy-tale, and that the listener will best do it justice by listening to it as a piece of music without trying to fit it to any collection of non-musical facts. As Weingartner has shrewdly pointed out, the main objection to fitting a piece of purely instrumental music to a chronological sequence of events is that different listeners will think at different paces, so that one will be in at the death of the Blatant Beast before another has discovered that the poem chronicles no such event. The shrewd Rimsky-Korsakov has prefixed Pushkin's introduction, which shows precisely the atmosphere of the work, but which just as definitely leaves the tale itself to the music. Here is a prose translation at two removes through the French translation of Dupont:

In a round place on the sea-shore there is a green oak: a golden chain hangs from the tree, and a wise cat is tied thereto and prowls round and round, night and day. When he goes to the right he hums a song—when to the left he tells a tale. There are marvels in that place: there a satyr wanders; there a naïad sits on the branches; there, in small, unknown pathways, appear the tracks of wondrous beasts; there you see, supported on hen's legs, a little cottage without doors or windows; there woods and vales swarm with ghosts by the thousand; there, at dawn, the tide beats on the desert sandy shore, and thirty splendid knights come out in line from the crystal waves, followed by their sea-tutor; there a young king, riding his ways, captures a terrible sovereign; there, in the clouds, in sight of the people, an enchanter carries off a hero over the woods and the seas; there, in her prison, a young queen sheds tears, having no servant and companion but a wolf who serves her faithfully; there King Kostchei perishes, staring at his gold; there dwells a Russian spirit . . . there all breathes Russia.

I have been there; I have drunk hydromel; I have seen the green oak by the sea; I have sat upon its roots, and the wise cat has told me his tales.

I REMEMBER ONE: AND HERE IT IS.

First there is a mysterious introduction; the quotation shows its two main figures, the one ominous in the basses, and the other querulous in the violins.

Ex. 1.
Larghetto.

Then, beneath sustained wailing harmonies, a slow fugue subject crawls up from the basses.

Ex. 2.

Eldritch squeals accompany its emergence into the upper regions; and then the harmony brightens into daylight, and the clarinet gives out a naïvely graceful melody, in Rimsky-Korsakov's invariable type of self-repeating two-bar phrasing. Here are the main figures:

Ex. 3.
(a)

(b)

&c.

(c)

The flowing accompaniment (b) is important in later developments, and so also is figure (c), which leads to a wistful sequel, which I have not space to quote; oboes and bassoons complaining above basses that ruminate on figures of Ex. 2, while violins answer with a mysterious new chattering figure leading back to the materials of Ex. 1. Suddenly the trombones burst out in grotesque tragedy.

Ex. 4.

The figures of Ex. 1 play a dramatic part in this catastrophe; and a new movement begins, with grim liveliness.

Ex. 5.
Allegretto.

As it proceeds, with increasing speed and excitement the figures of
Examples 1 and 4 are worked in; when suddenly the fury breaks off
into the plaintive (unquoted) sequel of Ex. 3, and a violin solo,
climbing down with the querulous second figure of Ex. 1, leads to
the following indolently whimsical dance-tune (or march) for the
flute—or for Pushkin's wise cat?

Ex. 6.

The continuation grows more and more capricious and rich in
modulation, culminating in a rhetorical pause; upon which the
clarinet, accompanied by the harp, enters with Ex. 3 in B flat and
transformed into 2/4 time. It works the tune up to a new and
happy climax and close. Then some of the lively material of Ex. 5
follows, with an exciting crescendo; the violins eventually bringing
in the 'chattering' figure mentioned among the sequels of Ex. 3.
This quickly brings about the triumphant outburst of Ex. 3 in the
full orchestra; and the trombones are quite spectacular in their
attack on the flowing accompaniment figure (Ex. 3 (b)). The
important figure (c) brings about a new turn of events, passing
into 6/4 time (which practically amounts to restoring the original
rhythm) and continuing in a new flow of melody, beneath which
the mysterious fugue-subject of Ex. 2 looms up in the basses. The
violins answer it, and then the accompaniment figure ((b) of Ex. 3)
breaks loose; and, after a catastrophic pause, the lively material of
Ex. 5 is resumed and worked up in more grotesque tragedy than
ever, the trumpets making wild mockery of Ex. 4. Again we have
the same turn of events; that is to say, the plaintive sequel of Ex. 3
intervenes and leads, in a new key (C sharp minor), to the whimsical dance-tune of Ex. 6; the flute and solo violin now exchanging
parts. Then we have again the melody of Ex. 3 in its 2/4 version;
this time as an oboe solo. The accompaniment figure (b) is given to
pizzicato violas, and it also flutters at double speed up and down in
the flute. A harp lets off rockets in the form of its characteristic
glissandos, an effect which is as fresh here as it was the day in 1880
when it was written. (When lesser composers cheapen such effects
they do so only in their own works: the poet who says the right
thing in the right place with conviction has nothing to fear from
those who have said it before or who shall say it afterwards.)
Once more, though only for a moment, the tune bursts out in

triumph with the full orchestra. Nothing except the scores of
Mozart can surpass the accuracy and variety of Rimsky-Korsakov's
orchestral economy. This fairy-tale, like all his operas and
orchestral works, has given out each of its many themes and
passages several times *in extenso*, and each time with a new per-
mutation of the whole set of parts. The balance of tone is always
perfect, the colour is always intensely brilliant and not less intensely
pure.

The plaintive continuation of Ex. 3 now intervenes tragically and
brings back the original slow tempo and themes of the opening, as
in Ex. 1. These work their way through mysterious chords to
a serene close in which the oboe gives the first bars of Ex. 3, while
the bell-like harmonics of the harp, beneath a solo violin, die away
in the accompanying figure (*b*).

'Here dwells a Russian spirit; here all breathes Russia.' Rimsky-
Korsakov is just the right master for the Russian fairy-tale: grotesque, with no clowning; ironic, with no lack of love; gorgeous
from childlike pleasure in bright colours, with no self-conscious
effort to make an impression; and, behind and above all the
grotesqueness, irony, and caprice, eminently attractive and innocent.
This specimen represents no more than his average, but it does
not deserve neglect.

PARRY

CLXXXIII. 'OVERTURE TO AN UNWRITTEN TRAGEDY'

I hope that the public will come to agree with me in gratitude to
Sir Adrian Boult for rediscovering one of the finest works of my
beloved master, Hubert Parry. I heard its first performance in
the 'nineties, and I confess with shame that I have only now studied
the score. Yet for me these thirty-odd years of neglect have
resulted in showing me this masterpiece in lights which I should
otherwise have missed. The score recalls vividly to me many
impressions of its first performance; amongst others, that it was
marked by the perfunctory efficiency which never rises beyond
the level of that skill in sight-reading for which British musicians
were already famous in the days of Wagner. I do not remember
the names of either orchestra or conductor; the hall was St. James's,[1]
and I am not sure that the Queen's Hall had then been opened. At
that time I fiercely resented the slightest criticism of my beloved
master's work; and when one of Parry's most loyal and distinguished colleagues remarked to me, 'I don't think the coda quite

[1] No; an obliging reader has kindly sent me the programme of the
occasion; it was at the Queen's Hall.

comes off', I saw no future for British music except to be stifled in wet blankets by its friends. Curiously enough, I now have a strong impression that the printed score has a different end from that which I heard then. I can trust none of these memories; so many of them drift into memories of later reflections on the subject; but I am almost certain that the resigned pathos of the coda, with its major mode, was retained to the end, and that the overture died away without a final outburst of energy.

It is surprising that Ex. 3, the main theme of the Allegro, is the only one that I remember, and that my memory of it is quite exact for the first bar and a half, that is, for the whole identifying clause. Two essential features of it are new to me, and from this I infer that the performance was as uncomprehending as the programme notes. The violent scoring of these shattering rhythms in massed chords, and the fierce accents in unexpected places, these are features that I surely would have remembered if the performance had done justice to them; and I cannot imagine that they are points added after revision.

Like Brahms's Tragic Overture, the influence of which it shows at no cost to its own independence, Parry's overture puzzled every one who believed that the word 'tragic' applies primarily to disasters that demand the attention of the police and secondarily to stage dramas in which the final curtain falls on the violent death of one or more persons who could never have been happy under any conceivable circumstances. The writer of those programme notes in the 'nineties seemed puzzled by the considerable differences between this *Overture to an Unwritten Tragedy* and the finale of Tchaikovsky's Pathetic Symphony. He quoted one passage in bustling semiquavers, and said, 'this, at all events, seems gay'. I have only a vague recollection of the 'look of the page' to help me to identify the 'gay' passage. It almost certainly was not Ex. 6; and the development opens with a quite mysterious semiquaver passage which recalls to me the 'look' of the quotation, but which is not thematic at all and which introduces, with appropriate dramatic suspense, one of the most pathetic parts of the whole work. Let no one imagine that those English composers of the 'nineties whom our iconoclasts dubbed 'proud academics' were a mutual admiration society that grew rich in the production of 'best sellers'. In the 'nineties anything like solid knowledge of musical composition was quite as much a persecuted heresy as it has been since; and the devotion of our 'proud academics' to the service of music was utterly unalloyed with any selfish aims or vanities.

Parry's overture begins with an introduction on a large scale. In Ex. 1 the bass and inner parts comprise in their first three notes a figure (*a*) which may be traced in many of the later themes—

Ex. 1.

For instance, out of that figure arises a contrasted cantabile beginning thus in F major—

Ex. 2.

and mounting in sequences to a tremendous climax which culminates in the fierce main theme of the allegro energico.

Ex. 3.

From this point the overture moves rapidly, instantly proceeding to a transition theme—

Ex. 4.

which rises to a great height of passion before subsiding pathetically, with an allusion to Ex. 1, figure (*b*), and closing into the second group.

The second group begins with a consolatory cantabile in C major—

Ex. 5.

the counterstatement of which leads to an animato theme—

Ex. 6.

which works up to a climax marked by a cadence theme—

Ex. 7.

This repeats itself with the usual cadential emphasis, **and,** after another noble climax, leads to a die-away end.

The final close is interrupted by a change of harmony, and the development begins with mysterious whisperings in the violins (is this the Victorian analyst's 'note of gaiety'?), which lead to a pathetic working-up of the inner figure (*a*) of Ex. 1, in the present tempo. The general tendency of the development is to assimilate the material of the introduction to the tempo and style of the allegro. Thus, after a short crescendo has led to an outburst of Ex. 3, the next event is a development of Ex. 2, which now leads to the recapitulation by a process similar to, but shorter than, that with which it led to the allegro.

The recapitulation is compressed but regular, giving in the tonic major almost the whole transition and the whole second group. But the cadence theme (Ex. 7), instead of leading to a climax and a die-away, leads to a dramatic catastrophe marked by a pause—

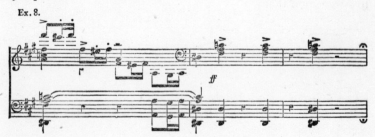

Ex. 8.

and followed (as the example indicates) by a deeply pathetic new development of figure (*b*) and other features of the introduction. Then the coda settles to a quiet *Verklärung* (transfiguration) suggestive (but not more than suggestive) of Ex. 5. But the climax that follows is concerned with the energetic themes, Exx. 3 and 7; and the final note of the overture, though solemn and in the major mode, is not that of peace, but of confidence that the battles which yet must come are worth fighting even if the only victory is death.

Parry's title for this noble work happily forbids us to find for it any more definite programme.

JULIUS RÖNTGEN

CLXXXIV. OLD NETHERLAND SUITE

1 *Janne moeie, al claer, al claer!* 2 *Niet dan druk en lijden en is in't herte mijn.* 3 *Contredans.* 4 *Heer Halewijn zong een Liedekijn.*

The main themes of the first two movements of this suite are from the composer's own *Amoreuse Liedekens*, op. 29, nos. 11 and 6. The other themes are national, and have become well known to all the world in Röntgen's pianoforte versions, which are in the repertoires of many eminent pianists, and especially in that of Mr. Percy Grainger.

Röntgen was one of the greatest musical scholars within the orbit of Brahms. His orchestration was as masterly as his pianoforte playing, and had no trace of the influence of the pianoforte which has so often cramped a composer's orchestral imagination. On the contrary, Röntgen's orchestration is a brilliant by-product of his extraordinary skill in counterpoint. The Netherlands was the early home of the most fantastic contrapuntal conjuring-tricks that the world has ever seen; and we need not be surprised that Röntgen had found Dutch melodies capable of combining with each other in all manner of ingenious ways. High spirits and an all-pervading sense of beauty animate Röntgen's work, whether he uses his own material or the themes of folk-song. The result always seems much simpler than it really is. The present work exemplifies a rule which great masters observe when they are going to give simple folk-music an elaborate treatment. The complete simple statement is given first: we are not detained by a lengthy and solemn process of mystification before the music makes its point. The first point is the tune 'Bonny Jean, all's ready, all's ready'.

Ex. 1.

The second point is the second tune.

Ex. 2.

This may have its own vagaries, such as a continuation in quick triple time (3/8); but there are no discussions and no digressions until the tunes are completed. After that, off they go into double fugue—

Ex. 3.

in which anything may happen and most things do.

The second movement ('Nought but heaviness and woe is in my heart') alternates two pathetic melodies—

Ex. 4.

and—

Ex. 5.

in a simple scheme which does not come to an end, but, pausing on a half-close, leads to a brilliant orchestration of a couple of dance-tunes very well known in Röntgen's pianoforte settings—

Ex. 6.

Big Drum.

and, with its *deux-temps* rhythm of 3/2 against 6/4—

Ex. 7.

The broad opening melody of the finale (Herr Halewijn sang a little song, and whoever heard it would fain be with him)—

Ex. 8.

becomes transformed in its accent by 'diminution' thus—

Ex. 9.

in which version it develops as a close figure, in combination at first with the original form (Ex. 8) and then, as quicker motion sets in, most surprisingly with Ex. 2, by means of which it brings the suite to a brilliant and sonorous end.

ELGAR

CLXXXV. VARIATIONS FOR ORCHESTRA, OP. 35

This delightful work, which first revealed to foreign nations that there was more mastery of orchestration, as well as of form, in British music than they were aware of, has been known, with the connivance of its composer, as the 'Enigma Variations'. One part of the enigma is, in a sense, musical, and I confess that I do not know its answer. The 'Enigma', as the theme is called, is said to be a counterpoint to a well-known tune which is not alluded to in the variations. This being so, the 'well-known tune' and the difficulty of guessing what it is are things that do not belong to the music as we have it. At all events I find nothing enigmatic in the composition, and until I do I shall not bother my head with an enigma which concerns no question of mine. Another part of the enigma is personal; and, as such, is the private affair of the composer and those friends of his whom it concerns. To them it is probably no enigma. The variations are 'Dedicated to my friends pictured within', and the evidently delightful people therein pictured are indicated by initials and pseudonyms. If there is one thing that music can clearly illustrate without ceasing to be musical, it is just this kind of character-drawing that is independent of narrative and concrete fact. At the same time if I were a policeman I think I should ask Mr. G. R. S. of variation 11 to produce his dog-licence; the behaviour of those basses paddling, with the theme, after a stick thrown into the pond by the violins, and the subsequent barking of the brass, can hardly be mere coincidence. Even so, the result is quite as musical as if there were no such things in nature. None of these externals detracts from the pure musical beauty and value of a work which has long taken rank as a permanent addition to the classical repertoire. No amount of practice wears it thin, and there is many an ambitious composer of brilliant and revolutionary reputation who ought to be taken by the scruff of his neck and, orchestrally speaking, washed in its crystal-clear scoring until he learns the meaning of artistic economy and mastery.

The theme, with its two contrasted strains in minor and major, is given in its essentials in the following quotation:

Ex. 1.

A. Da Capo.

The variations, with the partial exception of Var. 10 (Dorabella' and the Romance, Var. 13 (***), are all melodic; that is to say, it is the melody, and not essentially the structure or phrasing, which they reproduce. Where the melody is not recognizable, the composer's object is to give an independent episode, after the manner of Schumann's *Études Symphoniques*. These episodes are placed so as to relieve the melodic variations without breaking the coherence of the whole work.

Var. 1 (C. A. E.) is a beautiful glorification of the theme, which we shall encounter again in the finale. To quote Weber's *Oberon*, 'a gentle ray, a milder beam breaks sweetly on' phrase B of the theme when it is here removed to the softer key of E flat.

Var. 2 (H. D. S.-P.), in quick 3/8 time, begins with a fluttering staccato figure in dialogue with the violins, to which anxious harmonies soon enter wailing in the wind. Then the basses enter with A of the theme. When this is done, the fluttering figures are left behind, soon to vanish into darkness.

Var. 3 (R. B. T.) is a kind of mazurka, in the major mode and in a regular form with repeats. B, suddenly removed to F sharp major, is expanded to a climax from which the basses crawl with grotesque mystery back to the graceful, playful opening.

Var. 4 (W. M. B.), 3/4, in the minor again, storms through the whole theme in a violent temper which the feeble-forcible expostulations of a few frightened wood-winds only exasperate.

Var. 5 (R. P. A.), 12/8 and 4/4, in C minor, takes a gloomy view of A, in the bass with a sombre counterpoint in the violins. The flute runs away with B, which allies itself with a new tripping measure. This, however, does not prevail against the serious outlook, and the variation is dying away sadly, when—

Var. 6, 3/2, C major (Ysobel), who must, in her quiet way, be a perfect hostess, discusses the whole theme in a delightful dialogue, led by a solo viola and shared by all the nicest conversationalists in the orchestra. No tea-cup ever had a more delicate aroma than the last long note of the horn with the viola's last word below it: nor is there any exaggeration in calling the whole episode tone-poetry of an order far too high to be damaged by the lightness of its subject.

Var. 7 (Troyte), with his three drums, is as impossible at afternoon tea as Bernard Shaw's Professor Higgins was in his mother's drawing-room. But Pygmalion is a good fellow for all that.

Var. 8 (W. N.), 6/8, G major, restores peace and comfort with an exquisite epigrammatic neatness and amiability.

Var. 9 (Nimrod), 3/4, E flat, strikes a deeper note. The gay company of the others is not rebuked by it, for no one is hard or silly in this symposium; but the unworldly idealism of this new character is completely at home in its surroundings.

Var. 10 (Dorabella), 3/4, G major, is charming, fluttering, a little plaintive, and so constituted as to float inevitably into the middle of the picture.

Var. 11 (G. R. S.), 2/2, G minor, is the man I have already described as probably the owner of a lively retriever.

Var. 12 (B. G. N.) turns the theme into a melancholy serenade for the 'cellos. It leads to—

Var. 13 (***), Romance, a free episode which is indeed the most romantic thing in the work. The sound of a kettledrum-roll, beaten with side-drum-sticks, and the heaving swell of the violas are suggestive of the sea; and this confirms the rumour that the quotation-marks which the composer puts round the first phrase of the wonderful clarinet solo refer to Mendelssohn's overture, *Calm Sea and Prosperous Voyage*, the main theme of which contains the same familiar figure. To explain this typographical detail, however, is not to explain away the originality and depth of this most impressive passage.

Var. 14 (E. D. U.), the finale, rouses us with the approach of a spirited march. When this has reached the height of its course, there is a sudden dramatic stoppage. The wood-wind ask a question which turns out to be a prominent counterpoint in Var. 1 (C. A. E.). That seraphic and sympathetic being thereupon sails in with all its gentle radiance; and the march (the rhythms of which have accompanied this reappearance) resumes its course and rises to a climax which would be solemn but for its irrepressible tendency to hurry. This tendency increases, while the theme strides over the two-time bars in triple rhythm and the organ begins to boom in the background, until at last the great work rushes in semibreves to its cheerful end.[1] Written at the end of the nineteenth century, it had an immediate success which was no more than the twentieth century will deem a bare acknowledgement of its due. A work of the ripest mastery, it is a glorious beacon to the young composer in the storm and stress of ideas not newer than its own.

CLXXXVI. OVERTURE, 'COCKAIGNE', OP. 40

British music is emerging from various forms of darkness before dawn; and of these forms perhaps the darkest is that which a now almost too popular psychology calls 'the inferiority complex'. When, at the turn of the century, Elgar expressed his love of London in an overture neither more nor less vulgar than Dickens, the principal impression made on the musical criticism of those

---

[1] I am indebted to the original of Var. 8 for information correcting a rumour that the work was at first planned to end quietly. It had ended abruptly but not quietly, and the present coda was a necessary expansion.

ancient days was one of reverential dread at the audacity of an
English composer who handled the resources of sonata form as
if he had the presumption to understand them. There had been
British symphonic works in sonata form before; but orchestration
had not been our forte, and here was sonata form stated in terms
of consummate orchestration. This was clearly wrong; so clearly
that nobody could say why it was wrong. Hence it followed that
the work must be appallingly clever and complicated.

Even now, nobody can say why it is wrong. I believe some think
it vulgar. Nobody nowadays thinks it complicated. There were
people at the end of last century who thought Albert Chevalier's
songs vulgar; presumably because of their dialect. But vulgarity
in the ordinary (or vulgar) offensive sense lies not in dialects and
not in facts, but in errors of valuation. I cannot find vulgarity
in Elgar's Brass Band as it comes blaring down B flat Street, for
I see no evidence that he intends it to strike a religious note, or
a White Man's Burden note, or any note except the healthy note
of marching in good athletic form on a fine day. The *Cockaigne*
Overture is true to nature, and says its say straightforwardly in
terms of the highest art.

Its first theme, of which I quote only one phrase—

Ex. 1.

has a magnificent Cockney accent in that pause on the high C.
A further sequel anticipates (if my chronology is right) by some
years the vogue of the idiom of the Londoner who strongly affirms
that he does *not* think.

Ex. 2.

After a full orchestral counterstatement of Ex. 1, a new theme,
designated by Elgar's favourite mark, *nobilmente*, sounds a deeper
note.

Ex. 3.
Nobilmente.

Rude little street-boys, each conscious of being born with a Lord
Mayor's Mace up his back-bone, are apt, in later developments,
to whistle it away in irreverent diminution, as the *Lehrbuben* in

Meistersinger treat the theme of their masters; but at present its dignity is undisturbed.

There are quiet spaces in London, with room for lovers in sunshine and moonshine; and with these the second subject (in E flat) is concerned.

Ex. 4.

But it is also concerned with the irreverent diminishers of Ex. 3, and it has room for a climax based on Ex. 1. Other themes might well deserve quotation as the overture moves quietly to its development, but I have space only for the appearance of the brass band which, after various warnings in distant sounds, bursts round the corner, while all the bells chronicled in 'Oranges and Lemons' ring at random.

Ex. 5.

This conspicuous event is followed by the quietest and most poetic developments in the whole overture, passages as deep as any in all Elgar's works; and when the recapitulation arrives it is expanded with admirable freedom and resource. The brass band returns in C major; and the noble strains of Ex. 3, supported by the organ, lead to a brilliant abrupt end with Ex. 1.

RICHARD STRAUSS

CLXXXVII.   TONE-POEM (AFTER NICOLAUS LENAU). 'DON JUAN', OP. 20

The three early symphonic poems of Strauss—*Don Juan* (op. 20), *Macbeth* (op. 23), and *Death and Transfiguration* (op. 24)—are of a maturity which is perhaps more astonishing in *Don Juan* than in the other two. *Tod und Verklärung* has a greater reputation with concert-goers, mainly because its intention is obviously sublime and the sentiment of the subject-poem is popular. But it is, both in poem and in music, not without the boyish facilities which the sentimental public loves. The hero, dying in a garret, remembering his childhood, his ideals, the cruel, censorious world that forbade him to follow them, the glorious transfiguration itself, are none of them ideas that have cost an amiable burgess a moment's anxiety, or the author of the poem as much thought as Strauss, even in his youth, put into orchestrating a common chord. But the *Don Juan* of Lenau is a poem with ideas beyond echoes of Byron, and beyond ambition to shock the reader. And their spirit, with its health, its egotism, and its un-Byronic acceptance of the consequences, is realized by Strauss in a music which seems incredibly remote from that of the Good Boy of the Conservatoire displayed in the opus numbers before this opus 20. The form is entirely admirable; the invention of themes is vigorous and by no means easy to trace to its intellectual antecedents; and the orchestration remains unsurpassed by Strauss himself in later works, except in so far as his whole musical language has changed to something he would not have accepted in his youth. And there is not so much of this change as one is inclined to think. The orchestration of *Don Juan* shows in every particular the ripest results of experience. It is by no means without its difficulties, though they are never of the kind which, in later works designed for double-sized orchestras, relies on the safety of numbers and gives the players passages which are merely 'wild-cat' for the individual, but which Strauss explains as the 'al fresco' technique of the modern orchestra. Yet the technique of *Don Juan*, though not al fresco, is thoroughly modern: it shows no 'conservative' tendencies in relation to its materials.

The first theme might conceivably have derived its inspiration from Berlioz, and the erotic passages theirs from Wagner; but only as one statement of the truth is inspired by another. Rebecca West, protesting against the laudation of Byron, accuses him of 'that quality of vulgarity which is like an iron wall between those who possess it and any kind of experience; since they are preoccupied with the value which experiences fetch in the eyes of the world, they never get in touch with the essential qualities of their experiences, and hence never develop any qualities of their own'. That iron wall comes between the verbal poet of *Tod und Verklärung* and the possibilities of basing really first-hand music on his poem. There is no such barrier between Lenau and the young Strauss. Whatever room this or that work may allow for difference of opinion as to the firmness of the artist's purpose, mastery is mastery wherever it is to be found; and at twenty-five years of age Strauss has mastered the potentialities of Lenau's *Don Juan* with a vigour that makes one puzzled by the amiable personal loyalty which could blind him to the second-hand quality of Ritter's *Tod und Verklärung*.

With 'programme music', even when it is so naïve as Berlioz's, it is a mistake to attempt to refer the music to details. Either it coheres as music, or it does not. Descriptive sounds may be realistic enough to explain the incoherence on a lower plane than that of the music. More often, they may completely fail to do so, or may seem to explain something not intended, as when the old lady complimented Berlioz on the vividness with which his music represented 'Roméo arrivant dans son cabriolet'. It is not necessary to master the details of Lenau's poem, though if Strauss's music had been written for the stage it would (like Mozart's, Wagner's, or Puccini's) have had its counterpart for every gesture of the action, and every material object and colour seen or described. But Strauss's *Don Juan* is not stage music, and the three extracts he quotes from Lenau's poem are all that he wishes to lay before the public as a guide to the music. Study of the whole poem will be much more illuminating in the light of the music than study of the music in the light of the poem.

Don Juan says (in German hendecasyllables with double rhymes):

'Fain would I run the circle, immeasurably wide, of beautiful women's manifold charms, in full tempest of enjoyment, to die of a kiss at the mouth of the last one. O my friend, would that I could fly through every place where beauty blossoms, fall on my knees before each one, and, were it but for a moment, conquer. . . .'

'I shun satiety and the exhaustion of pleasure; I keep myself fresh in the service of beauty: and in offending the individual I rave for my devotion to her kind. The breath of a woman that is as the odour of spring to-day, may perhaps to-morrow oppress me like the air of a dungeon. When I in my changes travel with my love in the wide circle of beautiful women, my love is a different thing for each one: I build no temple out of ruins. Indeed, passion is always and only the new passion; it cannot be carried from this one to that; it must die here and spring anew there; and, when it knows itself, then it knows nothing of repentance. As each beauty stands alone in the world, so stands the love which it prefers. Forth and away, then, to triumphs ever new, so long as youth's fiery pulses race!

.　　.　　.　　.　　.　　.　　.　　.　　.　　.

'Beautiful was the storm that urged me on; it has spent its rage, and silence now remains. A trance is upon every wish, every hope. Perhaps a thunderbolt from the heights which I contemned, struck fatally at my power of love, and suddenly my world became a desert and darkened. And perhaps not,—the fuel is all consumed and the hearth is cold and dark.'

The philosophy of these sentiments is not good citizenship, but it is neither insincere nor weak. It is selfish, but not parasitic; and it cares nothing for support from other people's opinions. It doubts, without any interest in the doubt, whether the heights it has scorned really exist or, if existing, would concern themselves to censure it with a thunderbolt. The wrath of heaven and the natural burning out of the allotted stock of fuel are ends equally trivial and equally inevitable to a career urged onward by the tempest of its passion for beauty.

Lenau's Don Juan is slain in a duel by the avenger of one of his victims. Strauss's music unmistakably represents, amongst other things, Don Juan's actual death, and the themes could no doubt be identified with various characters in the poem. The Berliozian opening themes unquestionably represent Don Juan himself, in all his youthful manly vigour.

The three themes here quoted culminate in a superb gesture as of welcome to Love wheresoever it may be found.

The plaintive accents (*flebile*) which answer the gesture are met with mockery; but soon the expected miracle happens. If Strauss had been intending to write in classical sonata form, he could not establish more clearly the orthodox dominant for a second subject than he does in the glittering passage which (with the entry of a solo violin) leads to a long love-scene in B major developed from the opening of Ex. 4. Nor, if Berlioz had intended to convince his admirer of the realism of his representation of 'Roméo arrivant dans son cabriolet', could he have achieved anything more unmistakable than the way in which the 'cellos follow the climax of the passion by a dryly questioning entry of Ex. 1, in the mood of our superman '*fliehend Ueberdruss und Lustermattung*'.

The love-theme makes one wistful attempt to claim him, but soon he is storming away '*hinaus und fort nach immer neuen Siegen*'. The next episode begins with a theme full of bitter pathos—

answered by a wailing figure (again marked *flebile*) in the flute.
The second figure of Ex. 1 (bars 3 and 4) has something to say in
the matter, and soon the trouble is soothed, and the first figure of
Ex. 5 becomes a subdued accompaniment to a melody of intense
repose, given to the oboe (an outstanding revelation of the character
of that instrument) over a very dark and soft background, the
double-basses being divided in chords of four notes.

Ex. 6.

From this we are roused by a very noble theme.

Ex. 7.

It causes the utmost distress to the calm melody of Ex. 6, and soon
leads to fierce conflicts. Mockery is expressed by a new jingling
theme which I do not quote; and another figure—

Ex. 8.

rises into importance. Don Juan's other themes bring matters to
a fatal issue. His death in a duel is easily recognized in the music,
and wailing fragments from the developments of Ex. 4 are heard
over the reverberations of his fall. But—

> *Es war ein schöner Sturm, der mich getrieben.*

The orchestra revives the memories of his power and of what it is
not unjustifiable to dignify with the title of his ideals. The manly
themes, including Ex. 7 and Ex. 8, blaze up to an exalted climax
on a grand scale. Suddenly the light fails—

> *der Brennstoff ist verzehrt*
> *Und kalt und dunkel ward es auf dem Herd.*

BANTOCK

CLXXXVIII. 'DANTE AND BEATRICE', POEM FOR ORCHESTRA

The subject of this tone-poem is, as the title implies, biographical,
and is not, like Liszt's Dante Symphony, a musical illustration of
the *Divina Commedia*. Nor, on the other hand, is it restricted to
exact chronological sequence. Its course is that of a straight-

forward orchestral piece full of rich tone-colour, and inspired in
its changes and unities by the character of Dante as it appears in
the story of his life and work.

I have the authority of the composer for the external ideas which
are here attached to this and that feature of this musically self-
explanatory piece.

The first and principal theme, introduced by three bars on the
drums, expresses the personality of 'Dante—sombre and stern'.

Ex. 1.

Maestoso dolente.

Drums.

Its first exposition is in the manner of an extensive introduction,
towards the end of which another theme (among several) appears
that should be noted, as it anticipates, like a tragic longing for
something as yet unknown, the themes of Beatrice.

Ex. 2.

&c.

This introduction plunges into a stormy section, beginning with
Ex. 1 in a more solid form, and passing to developments representing 'Times of Strife; Guelfs and Ghibellines'. An impassioned
canonic development of Ex. 1 demands quotation here—

Ex. 3.

&c.

The simpler and more drastic sounds of strife may speak for
themselves. Throughout, the character of Dante remains unyield-
ing. A climax is reached in which the whole orchestra is opposed
to the drums in violent rhythms interrupted by bars of silence.

Then comes the miracle of Dante's meeting with Beatrice. A
harp is heard in alternation with the recitatives of a solo violin.
In the second part of the example (overleaf) we may identify
Beatrice herself.

Ex. 4.

And in Ex. 5 we may suppose the commotion aroused in Dante at his first sight of her, and dominating all his thoughts, until he was launched upon his project to write of her that which had never yet been written of any woman.

Ex. 5.

With a return to agitated developments of the former material, the music begins to deal with the *Divina Commedia*. Here it will save trouble to note that the tone-poem rests upon two key-centres, that of C minor, for Dante and his earthly troubles, and its flat supertonic D flat major, for Beatrice and the Beatific Vision. The whole music is derived, with tenacious logic, from previous material, as if to show that Dante's Vision was the mirror of his earthly life. One violent incident, which occurs twice, may be quoted here.

Ex. 6.

By degrees the passionately longing figure of Ex. 2 gains more and more ascendancy, and its tonality approaches ever nearer to the D flat region associated, like the figure itself, with Beatrice. In D flat all the main themes (Ex. 3; the first bars, but not the rest, of Ex. 4; and Ex. 5) are united in an impassioned climax, the tragic catastrophe of which leads to a dark fugue indicating Dante's exile.

Ex. 7.

From this point however, while there is plenty of rich modulation, there is no swerving from the tonality and mood of Beatrice, and we are allowed to hear again the second part of Ex. 4, developed in full glory; until at last the glory becomes suddenly remote and yet all-pervading, and all the hierarchies of Heaven are seen with every soul in its place in the mystic Rose whose centre is God.

J. B. McEWEN

CLXXXIX. 'GREY GALLOWAY', A BORDER BALLAD FOR FULL ORCHESTRA

From the composer I learn that there is no legend to serve as 'programme' to this piece of pure music. It is called a ballad, as certain compositions by Chopin are called Ballades. Galloway is merely a geographical expression, and not a Laird or Younger of that ilk; and 'grey' refers to the weather that prevailed there in the September when the composer conceived this work—if not also at other times.

Certain features of the music are intimately Scottish. For example, the lovers of folk-music who think that 'Annie Laurie' is a folk-song, have probably forgotten or never known that the pentatonic scale has a mode for each of its notes. The opening theme of *Grey Galloway* is not a folk-song, but it is a typical example of pentatonic Dorian, in the scale D F G A C D.

Ex. 1.

In complete contrast to this, the first episode, in the remote key of B major, gives an impression of fairy-like subtleties of sunlight and gossamer-strewn heather seen through rain and mist.

Ex. 2.

This may not have been the composer's idea; but it is about the sort of thing I should represent by such scoring if I wanted to write descriptive music. As Mendelssohn once pointed out in an amazingly clever letter, it is music that has the definite meaning for musical people, and words that mean different things in different mouths.

Rondo-like, the first theme returns. A second episode is in a pentatonic Phrygian mode E G A C D E.

Ex. 3.

Sea-birds seem to be hovering in the air, until the misty grey darkens.

IV   M

When this episode has slowly died away there is a sound of hurrying crowds. While the sound is low, distant, and indistinct, it might be thought menacing; but the crowd enters the scene with nothing more dangerous than a Hornpipe.

Ex. 4.

Being inexpert in such matters I will not commit myself to the assertion that this is a Hornpipe; for I am not sure that it may not be a Reel, though I think it is definitely not a Strathspey. For all I know, it may be a Highland Fling. Or it may be the dance that Bishop Grocote danced with the cook in *Stronbuy*, after the Free Kirk minister had called him a Dissenter. At all events all these dances, though not dangerous, are exciting; and this one makes a brilliant end to a piece which has made a large number of vivid contrasts out of its Gallowegian greys. At last the Hornpipe (I am almost sure that it is a Hornpipe) shows its kinship with Ex. 1 by the following theme, which is what textual critics would call a conflation of the two.

Ex. 5 (*cf.* Ex. 1).

And so the work ends with a return to the figures of its first bars. There are several important figures besides the five here quoted; but those unquoted concern finer detail than this analysis attempts to show.

ERNEST WALKER

CXC. FANTASIA—VARIATIONS ON A NORFOLK FOLK-SONG, OP. 45

This work was written in November 1929 as a pianoforte duet. Like all four-hand pianoforte music, it is full of matter for orchestration; and the orchestral version, written ten months later, has all the point of an original composition. Two themes underlie the whole: the theme of the Variations, a tune entitled 'Lovely Joan' collected by Vaughan Williams at Acle, Norfolk, and published in No. 15 of the Folk-song Society's Journal; and a motto on the notes A G A E D, which are the musical letters in the name of a friend, used as Schumann used the various musical spellings of A S C H in his *Carnaval*.

An introduction meditates on the first three notes of 'Lovely Joan' (Ex. 1, figure (a)), in conjunction with developments of the name-theme.

Ex. 1.

A clarinet quotes the cadence of Mendelssohn's *Calm Sea* that Elgar glorified in the Romance of his *Enigma* Variations, and this brings the introduction to a crisis and a pause.

The variation theme is in two strains, and is stated by an oboe and bassoon in octaves, with modal harmonies added at the cadences. It begins as follows:

Ex. 2.

This is half of the first strain, and is an admirable specimen of pure Dorian mode. The second strain rises to the octave. It is repeated, with primitive but modern harmonization.

The variations are free in form, but clear in their melodic derivation from the theme. In the first variation the violins enter with an impulsive uprush, and the figures of the theme are developed through a flow of semiquavers. The energy subsides abruptly, and the variation floats away in a dramatic diminuendo.

The second variation quietly accompanies the theme with counterpoint in quavers.

The third variation harmonizes the melody in C major without transposing it. The scoring is full and loud, with triplet quaver counterpoint.

The fourth variation, entering after an impressive sustained pianissimo chord of C on horns, first muted and then opened, is a very quiet adagio in the remote key of E flat major. The return from this to E minor is by a very fine abrupt modulation.

The fifth variation is in the home tonic and in 3/4 time. It rises to a climax, before dying away into an intermezzo variation in common time, which leads to a new harmonization (Var. 7) of 'Lovely Joan' with the name-theme above it as an ostinato in cross rhythm.

Ex. 3.

The ostinato lasts through both strains of the tune, and subsides only when the second strain is repeated. Then new modulations lead to a peaceful eighth and last variation in E major. At the end the name-theme descends in sequences thus to a serene close—

Ex. 4.

VAUGHAN WILLIAMS

CXCI. OVERTURE TO 'THE WASPS'

The plays of Aristophanes give the composer abundant opportunities for music; and Vaughan Williams has made brilliant use of those afforded by *The Wasps*. Besides the choruses, which are restricted and inspired by the elaborate precision of Greek metrical forms, there is material in the incidental music for an effective orchestral suite. Of this the overture, to be performed on the present occasion, is the largest and most developed movement. I have not at hand the means of assigning its various themes to precise functions in the Aristophanic drama, nor is this aspect a matter of Wagnerian importance. The Athenians, according to the play, were going through a phase of litigious mania, for which the demagogue Cleon was largely to blame. Law-suits have bereft poor old Philocleon of whatever wits he once had, and he makes his entry up through the chimney, explaining that he is the smoke. His son Bdelycleon can keep him quiet only by occupying him with the trial of a dog, with counsel for prosecution and defence, pathetic exhibition of the wailing about-to-be dispossessed or orphaned puppies, &c., all complete. The chorus, appropriate to the Athenian temper, is a chorus of wasps.

The overture accordingly presents a compendium of Aristophanic matters, of which the main sentiment is that the Athenians are good-natured healthy enough people, if only they would not allow demagogues to lead them by the nose. Accordingly, apart from the normal Gregorian tones of a wasps' nest, the music

consists of a brilliant scheme of tunes galore, in the style of folk-
songs, diatonic by nature, but occasionally inveigled by Cleon into
a whole-toned scale. I am not interested to know which, if any,
of these tunes are actual folk-melodies. Vaughan Williams ranks
with Marjorie Kennedy-Fraser among the supreme discoverers
and recorders of genuine folk-music; but he can invent better
tunes than any that will ever be discovered by research. And if he
himself were to tell me that there were pantomimic topical allusions
to Aristophanes in the original folk-poems of his tunes, I fear I
should be strongly tempted to extemporize additions to such
details until my whole analysis became a 'leg-pull'. The listener
may be further reassured on another point. The music owes
nothing to researches for ancient Greek musical fragments; its
archaisms are the latest (or nearly the latest) modernisms of a lover
of British folk-music, and it has no tendency to base 'We won't go
home till morning' on the supertonic of a minor key, and sing it
in five-eight time, thus—

as is the way of composers too learned in ancient Greek music.[1]
Here, then, are the main themes of this overture. First a rowdy
couple of dance-measures, with a tendency to combine in primitive
counterpoint.

Ex. 1.

Ex. 2.

Lastly, a gentle, broad melody first stated by itself in E flat and,
in the final stage of the movement, combined as follows with Ex. 1.

Ex. 3.

[1] This diatribe is emphatically not directed against the wonderful
ancient Greek melody so beautifully used in Ethel Smyth's *The Prison*.
I will not stir up wasps' nests by explaining what it is directed against.

REGER

CXCII. FOUR TONE-POEMS AFTER BÖCKLIN, OP. 128

1 *Der geigende Eremit* (*The Hermit with the Violin*). 2 *Im Spiel der Wellen* (*Among the Play of the Waves*). 3 *Die Toteninsel* (*The Isle of the Dead*). 4 *Bacchanal*.

When Reger's *Böcklin Suite* was published in 1913, Böcklin was considered fairly modern and by no means out of fashion. The anti-romantic reaction of the last twenty years has so diminished the market for reproductions of his pictures that even in his native Switzerland my friends have had much difficulty in providing information about these subjects of Reger's 'programme music'. Probably 'Die Toteninsel' is the only Böcklin picture that all British concert-goers will find familiar, though possibly 'Der geigende Eremit' ('The Hermit with the Violin') may also be familiar to many. It is perhaps hardly an over-statement to say that 'Die Toteninsel' is as constant an adornment of German lodgings as 'The Soul's Awakening' or 'The Stag at Bay' in English lodgings. Some allowance must be made for the fact that, in other arts besides music, German popular taste is less naïve than in this country, and that within living German memory royal patronage of the fine arts has been not only widespread, but multiplied by decentralization. In Great Britain, the decline of aristocratic support for the fine arts began with the abolition of that useful institution, the Heptarchy. Be this as it may, at the time when Reger wrote the *Böcklin Suite*, all the four pictures which it purports to illustrate were familiar to everybody and available in reproductions. Now my friends can procure me postcards of only three. I dare say that I shall recognize the 'Bacchanal' if and when I see it; but, after comparing the music of the other three with the pictures, I do not believe that Böcklin's 'Bacchanal' will throw much light upon Reger's brilliant and spirited finale. My formula for most cases of programme music is that for me the music throws more light upon the subject than the subject can throw upon the music; but this applies only to the work of attentive artists. I had rehearsed Reger's representation of 'The Hermit with the Violin' several times with great enjoyment of its mystical Phrygian tonality and its antiphonies of muted and unmuted strings; until at last I began dimly to remember the picture of a friar with a long white beard standing before some sort of shrine with bowed head, and playing on a violin. It is of no importance that I did not remember that he is standing in a sort of lean-to, but it is manifestly of great importance that he has an audience of infant angels, two of whom are perched in the window above him, while the third is standing

on tiptoe on the ground, looking through some kind of hole in the
wall. I am sceptical about the power of any music to suggest even
these important features to a listener who knows only the title of
the picture. Moreover, I am not at all confident that I can associate,
or that Reger would wish me to associate, any details of his music
with these pictorial features, now that I know them. There can
be no doubt that the mood of the picture is reproduced. A violin
is ruminating softly above and amid an orchestral design in the
Phrygian mode and full of mysterious whisperings. What more
Reger can do to illustrate the details of the picture, I am not on
reflection able to say. The angels' wings do not flutter, for this
would indicate flight. Moreover, what could be more calculated
to impart flight to infant angels and purgatorial penalties to composers and analysts than an attempt at further explanation?

Here is the opening theme: if the listener identifies it on its
return he will have grasped all that he needs to know about the
form of this tone-picture.

Ex. 1.

The music of 'Im Spiel der Wellen' has some, but not much,
affinity with the *Jeux des Vagues* in Debussy's *La Mer*. It is
much less elaborate in orchestration, but essentially not much
less impressionistic. There are several themes, and the listener
can use his fancy in associating loud and lively horn-themes with
shaggy male figures, such as the two in Böcklin's picture, and more
delicate themes, such as one in the middle of the piece:

Ex. 2.

with the female bathers. The big wave which is the central feature
of Böcklin's picture is easy to recognize. Note that Debussy's
piece is *Jeux des Vagues*, and, like the rest of *La Mer*, concerned
only with the waves themselves. Reger follows Böcklin, though
the title of the picture means the same as Debussy's title; but the
picture and Reger's music illustrate play *in* the waves, as well as
of the waves. Böcklin's little joke consists in making mermaids

and mermen out of ordinary human beings; and what is certainly
meant to look like the tail of a mermaid resolves itself, on closer
inspection, to the legs of a lady taking a header. (No marks will
be given to students of Form who identify this with Reger's casual
treatment of some figure or other by inversion.)

'The Isle of the Dead' is the picture that has made the name of
Böcklin a household word over all the world. I have neither talent
nor practice in describing pictures or their subjects. But I presume
that everybody will remember the majestic mass of perpendicular
rocks hollowed out in front by a space in which tall cypresses
overtop the rocks and conceal the back of the space. A low wall of
great uncemented stones runs in front of the space and is broken
in the middle by an entrance, towards which a boat is proceeding.
In the boat an upright figure stands with bowed head over a
coffin that is draped by what, if I mistake not, is a flag.

The picture has more form than Reger's music; but I am by
no means sure that the total contents of the music are less than
those of the picture: or, to put my opinion in clearer terms, I am
not sure whether if I knew anything about painting, I should not
rate Reger's 'Toteninsel' higher than Böcklin's. A more definite
comparison is futile. Böcklin is famous for his subtle handling
of blues. A philosopher has given as an example of indisputable
propositions the dictum that 'the soul is either blue or not blue'.
This does not help us. But the soul of this or that music is either
emotional or not emotional; and if Reger's 'Toteninsel' has been
inspired by Böcklin's picture it has been inspired by a powerful
emotion, and it achieves pathos of the highest order. I need not
quote themes. The beginning demands acute attention because it
is not only mysterious, but extremely soft. The emotional appeals
are sudden and overwhelming, especially when the music settles
down in its home tonic major, as if in reconcilement with the
fate of all mortals.

Of Böcklin's 'Bacchanal' I have been unable to obtain either a
reproduction or a detailed verbal description. But I understand
that it represents classical bacchants, satyrs, and fauns, in a
manner that does not explain itself away as do the marine folk of
'Im Spiel der Wellen'. At all events, it is important to realize that,
whatever the contents of Böcklin's 'Bacchanal', Reger's is not to be
rationalized into tavern orgies or town carnivals. For that matter,
when Böcklin himself, in his 'Im Spiel der Wellen', rationalizes his
mermaids and mermen, his point is rather to mythologize his
human bathers. Listen, then, to Reger's Bacchic orgy and let
your attention rouse your visual fancy to respond to the power of
his music to express the various phases of Bacchic frenzy, with
all its abrupt contrast, climaxes, darknesses, and hints of panic

terror, half-human fauns and satyrs, with a divine if dangerous power overruling all; and with the opening theme—

Ex. 3.

and the brilliant final climax for its high lights.

GUSTAV HOLST

CXCIII. BALLET FROM 'THE PERFECT FOOL', OP. 39

It is night. The Wizard is commanding the Spirits of Earth, Water, and Fire to bring him the wherewithal for the making of a magic potion. It will look and taste like pure water. If a woman drinks it, it is but water. If a man drinks it, his eye becomes all-powerful, compelling the love of women and slaying the foeman with a blast of fire. With the dawn of to-morrow the Princess is to choose a husband. Concerning her it has been prophesied that she shall marry the man that does the deed no other can do. Surely the Wizard, when he has drunk the potion, will be the man in question! (But his plans did not take account of the Perfect Fool, nor of the Perfect Fool's Mother.)

First the Wizard summons the Spirits of the Earth.

Ex. 1.

Spirits of the Earth,   Come at my call! ؛ ؛ O-bey my voice.

They come from the depths, like Nibelungs, bringing the magic cup which is to hold his potion.

Ex. 2.

Next he summons the Water-Spirits, that they may fill the cup with essence of pure consuming love—

Ex. 3.

(This passage will become a *locus classicus* for limpid orchestral colouring obtained with the simplest materials.)

The Water-Spirits move gently, and eventually subside in the tune the Princess will sing when she comes at early morn to choose her husband (overleaf)—

Ex. 4.

Lastly, the Wizard summons the Spirits of Fire that they may enter into the potion for the blasting of enemies. Their music requires no melodic quotation. Once it has blazed forth, nothing can stop its course as it tramps onward over an ostinato bass

while the lighter rhythms flicker above and sometimes accumulate in big flames—

At last it dies down, and the Salamanders, having fulfilled the Wizard's last command, disappear. The Wizard is weary. He sleeps, until the coming of the Perfect Fool and his astute Mother.

A. VOORMOLEN

CXCIV. OVERTURE, 'BARON HOP'

This overture is the prelude to a Choregraphical Fantasia dealing with the character (and capers) of Baron Hop, who was Ambassador of the Austrian Netherlands at the court of Stadtholder William V at the Hague in 1794. In the fourteenth edition of the *Encyclopædia Britannica* no biographical article intervenes between that on Hoover and the series of articles on the Hop in its botanic integrity and in its relation to beer. Important and august as these subjects are, they ought not to have crowded out so distinguished a person as the inventor of the Haagsche Hopjes. Nobody with the smallest pretensions to taste can travel in Holland without inwardly digesting these masterpieces of the 18th-century diplomat. To describe them as a form of toffee would impel Lord Chesterfield and his Netherland compeers (for Holland is a land of Chesterfields no less than pictures) to rise from their graves in a last forlorn hope that their protests might yet check for a while the descent of the world into a chaos of universal vulgarity.

That chaos is upon us already to this extent, that the modern traveller is confronted at every turn with the assertion that *this* firm (whose name eludes my memory) and no other is in possession of the genuine recipe of Baron Hop. To discuss these trade disputes were an un-Chesterfieldian task. Fortunately Mr. Voormolen is an artist who can produce genuine Haagsche Hopjes

(*scilicet* ballets) in a higher category than was dreamt of by Chesterfield; and in this overture we unquestionably have the genuine
article. In his own country this is attested not only by the fact
that the work is a popular item in great request at orchestral
concerts, but by the conspicuous absence of any attempt to attack
it on the part of rival manufacturers of the comestible.

The themes, the composer tells me, are mostly old Dutch songs
in praise of the House of Orange at the time of Baron Hop's career.
The word 'praise' is elastic, and it sometimes has to put up with
changes of tempo that may mislead people who do not move exclusively in exalted circles. Thus 'Hail Columbia, Queen of Nations'
is a very solemn tune when it is played in its proper hymn-like
minims. But it is better known in quavers as 'Yankee Doodle'.
Perhaps a similar transformation may have transformed the praise
of the House of Orange to the following remarks. I do not understand Dutch; but I should gather from the scoring and general
treatment that they were scurrilous.

Ex. 1.

Nor does the next theme, which becomes very important in later
developments, show any more signs of reverence.

Ex. 2.

A gavotte in A flat, which enters at an early stage of the exposition,
is above suspicion.

Ex. 3.

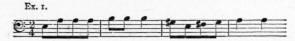

It is allowed to complete a graceful paragraph without interruption;
but then Ex. 2 breaks in with the most irreverent modulations.
Another hymn of praise intervenes. From its melody you would
think it to be in F sharp major—

Ex. 4.

but that is the one key in which its harmonies are certainly not.
Where else they may be is a secret like that of the genuine Haagsche
Hopjes. Many ingredients go to the making of even ordinary toffee.

These four themes, with a pinch or two of other substances,

having now been assembled, are thoroughly stirred together. Ex. 2 is apt to become augmented; and there is another lively tune, unquoted here, which also becomes augmented; an incident that may be recognized by the 'unison' of the piccolo and contrafagotto. The central climax of the overture is marked by the solemn triumphal entry of—

Ex. 5.

No; this is not the Marseillaise. Similarly, the Republic of Venice was not governed by a dog; the word is differently spelt.

The Marsollandaise having made its point, the confection is quickly stirred up to its final consummation. It ends with Ex. 2 in B flat, after a career in which keys have been relative in a somewhat Einsteinian way. Otherwise the harmony is by no means ultra-modern. The fun, the wit, and the art, different aspects of the same thing, are all musical and sane.

PAUL HINDEMITH

CXCV. CHAMBER MUSIC NO. 1, FOR SMALL ORCHESTRA, OP. 24, NO. 1

1 *Very quick and wild.* 2 *Moderately quick minims in very strict time.* 3 *Quartet: very slow and with expression.* 4 FINALE. 1921 : *extremely lively.*

Hindemith's music, even in his earlier works, will sound strange to many listeners. It is a severely disciplined art and rests upon massive and extensive theoretical foundations. The listener is not concerned with the theory, and those who know least either about it or about the theories of classical music are perhaps most likely to appreciate its effect. Some part of the theory may be summed up in the blessed if not Mesopotamian words 'polytonal' and 'atonal'.[1] 'Atonal' music is music to which you cannot assign either a key or a mixture of keys. 'Polytonal' music is music in which several voices or instruments are performing, each con-sistently in a separate key of its own. What the naïve listener needs to know about atonal music is the fact, demonstrated for all time by Lewis Carroll, that it takes a trained logician to write good nonsense. As to polytonal music, the person trained in the theory, as distinguished from the enjoyment, of classical music is apt to try and make sense of the chords produced at each moment. The naïve listener is much more likely to hear the simple fact that several people are playing in different keys at once. Not long ago I

---

[1] No, it may not. Hindemith, in his newly published *Unterweisung im Tonsatz*, emphatically denies the validity of atonality and polytonality. The following remarks apply therefore only to Modern Music.

had the pleasure of listening to Beethoven's Eighth Symphony, which is in F, accurately balanced against Haydn's Military Symphony in G, when our portable wireless got two foreign stations at once. The two symphonies remained perfectly distinct. One could hear either against the background of the other, but it was a psychological impossibility to combine them in one discordant mass.

The polytonal composer is less ambitious and more scrupulous. He does not pit whole symphonies against each other, and he does not produce his effects by accident. Sometimes he is merely doubling a melody in a consistent interval, whether concordant or discordant. Usually when people sing in thirds and sixths they are singing in the same key, and some of the sixths or thirds will be major and some minor, according to their position in the scale. Polytonality begins when, instead of this procedure, the two voices sing precisely the same melody in keys a third or a sixth apart. A discordant interval will do just as well. When the process is not one of doubling, but of actual polyphony (that is to say, when the melodies are different), the polytonal composer is impelled to his procedure by the experience that in classical polyphony a combination of melodies simply disappears as such. All that the listener appreciates at any moment is the top part and a general sensation of euphony and organization. The polytonal composer wishes to return to the more naïve experience of appreciating the fact that the performers are doing several different things. To the Oriental ear, unaccustomed to Western polyphony, there is very little difference between the most advanced things in modern music and the polyphony of Palestrina. It is impertinent to tell the conservative music-lover, who by fine sensibility and experience has come to understand classical music, that he ought to like polytonality and atonality; but he may be respectfully corrected if he argues that these modern tendencies are undisciplined or easy for the composer. In polytonality it is often as difficult as the strictest counterpoint to keep the different planes of key from undesired contact. And the most conservative critic may bless polytonality for having removed from the modern musician all possibility of the chromatic slush that started with poor honest, broad-minded Spohr and drew its glistening snail-track over the chords—lost, stolen, and strayed—of later nineteenth-century music.

It is usual to begin the criticism of a modern composer by speculating about his ultimate position in history. When this custom has become obsolete, musical criticism will have some chance of uttering a few sensible remarks. The present age will be like every other age in the history of the fine arts, in that a small fraction of one per cent. of what is now most talked about will be not only talked about but enjoyed a hundred or two hundred years hence. Of this I am quite sure, but I am not going to be such a fool as to say which works of the present day will belong to that percentage. Posterity has hitherto done nothing for me that should oblige me to bother about its judgement. I know what I like, and I know what bores me; and I am at present quite satisfied to know that I like Hindemith and that he does not bore me. As far as I can judge, his music does not bore many people, though it annoys some. He is never very long, he thumps no tubs, and his attitudes are not solemn. He is manifestly humorous, and he makes the best of modern life. Professor Saintsbury retained to his last days a hospitable mind, but among tendencies in modern art he drew the line firmly at two things. One of these he called 'bad blood', and the other 'rotting'. Both are as impossible to Hindemith as to an athlete. His music is at least as serious as a game, and that is something far more serious than anything that can put on solemnity as a garment. Neither with Hindemith nor with Haydn can I undertake to preserve a solemn countenance while I discuss their works, but I hope that none of my irreverent digressions will leave the reader in any doubt as to the importance of the subject.

As the term *Kammermusik* implies, we do Hindemith's Opus 24, No. 1, some violence in performing it in a large concert-hall. The work requires eleven players, one of whom, the person in charge of the *Schlagzeug* or percussion, is to 'serve' (as Hindemith puts it) nine instruments. The other instruments are: a flute, who sometimes turns into a piccolo, a clarinet, a bassoon, a trumpet, two violins, a viola, a 'cello, double-bass, pianoforte, and harmonium. The 'servant' of nine has to deal with a xylophone, a side-drum, a Holztrommel (a Chinese block-drum; or the head of a professor), a small pair of cymbals, a tambourine, a triangle, a tin canister full of sand, a siren, and one note of a glockenspiel. These mysteries would doubtless be more effective if we could respect the composer's recommendation that the players should be invisible to the public. This cannot be managed in a large hall with galleries; nor does the alternative that has been suggested by an untrustworthy critic commend itself; that, on the contrary, spotlights should be directed on the players, while the audience should be provided with the late Herbert Spencer's patent ear-stoppers. The canister full of sand has, I am informed, sometimes presented difficulty, owing to the fact that the sand obtainable from the grocer is so frequently adulterated with sugar; but in Edinburgh it is convenient to import the finest West Indian sand from Portobello.

It would be a great mistake to suppose that, because some of the sounds produced by this varied but not very large apparatus are strange and vague, anything impressionist or improvisatorial can be admitted in the performance. The composer himself is a master of several instruments and plays classical music like an angel; and his own music is, at its strangest, of such a quality that, after practising it, one returns to the study of classical music with all one's standards raised. Just as I thought I had exhausted the stock of jibes at Hindemith's experiments, I recollected that it is the correct thing to say that his humour and glitter is 'metallic'. This should have been said long ago of a good deal of stuff I could mention which is much more fashionable. It is quite untrue of Hindemith. To the credit of modern music-lovers, Hindemith's career is conspicuously successful. Fashionable it has not been; but his humour would have been fashionable enough if it had been metallic.

The listener must not expect too much help from an analysis. The most experienced score-reader would be little the wiser if I gave quotations from the opening movement, *sehr schnell und wild*. It is a short movement, alternating between a shrill bickering motive in a treble region around F sharp, and deeper pentatonic objurgations around and about C on the fourth string of the violins. It ends with a universal glissando and a bump, and serves as a short introduction to the second movement, which is a kind of march with the following main theme:

Ex. 1.

This quotation will suffice for the whole movement, which, though not long, cheerfully marches through a considerable range of picturesque musical scenery, while sticking closely to its theme.

The third movement is a quartet for flute, clarinet, bassoon, and one note of a glockenspiel. As cheerfulness broke in upon the philosophy of Dr. Johnson's friend Edwards, so romance breaks in upon the athletic severity of Hindemith; the fact of course being that true romance has no school and no opposition to the things which become classical, but is, as the late Sir Walter Raleigh used to say, the sense of 'something round the corner'. And so Hindemith allows his quartet to be not only '*sehr langsam*' but '*mit Ausdruck*', and even prescribes '*sehr zart*' (very tender) for the delivery of his main theme:

Ex. 2.

I am unable to specify what events of 1921 are referred to in the Finale. Many things were happening in all parts of the world at that day, and the summary of German history in the *Encyclopædia Britannica* does not give me any definite clue. The Finale begins with exciting and mysterious crowd-noises over a pianoforte bass which gradually accumulates broken rhythms into a pattern. The following themes emerge:

Ex. 3.

Ex. 4.

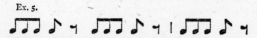

and are piled up by cumulative sequence in a crescendo. With various ups and downs the whole movement is, in fact, a crescendo, which, punctuated by a rhythmic figure, Ex. 5—

Ex. 5.

culminates in the entry of the trumpet with a fox-trot by Wilm Wilm. As Hindemith has had to obtain the permission of the publishers to use this fox-trot, I had better not quote it here. It is a good tune and not more difficult to follow than fox-trots usually are, though I doubt if Herr Wilm Wilm ever imagined his fox-trot in G accompanied by major scales simultaneously on all the other eleven keys of the octave.

The Finale ends with a *stretto* in quicker time, in which the fox-trot looms up from the bass until it reaches the treble. Sir Thomas Browne intelligently anticipated the final cadence of this work by stating that 'what song the sirens sung' is among the questions not wholly beyond conjecture. (See our catalogue on p. 174.)

SET IN GREAT BRITAIN AT THE UNIVERSITY PRESS OXFORD.
BY JOHN JOHNSON PRINTER TO THE UNIVERSITY
PRINTED BY MERRITT AND HATCHER, LTD., LONDON.